THE COLLEGE PRESS NIV COMMENTARY

1 & 2 PETER

THE
COLLEGE
PRESS
NIV
COMMENTARY

1 & 2 PETER

ALLEN BLACK
1 Peter

MARK C. BLACK
2 Peter

New Testament Series Co-Editors:

Jack Cottrell, Ph.D.
Cincinnati Bible Seminary

Tony Ash, Ph.D.
Abilene Christian University

COLLEGE PRESS
PUBLISHING COMPANY
Joplin, Missouri

Library of Congress Cataloging-in-Publication Data

Black, Allen, 1951–
    1 & 2 Peter/Allen Black, Mark C. Black.
      p. cm. — (The College Press NIV commentary)
    Includes bibliographical references.
    ISBN 0-89900-648-5 (hardcover)
    1. Bible. NT. Peter—Commentaries. I. Black, Mark C. (Mark
Cothran), 1956–   . II. Title. III. Title: First and Second Peter.
IV. Series.
BS2795.3.B55 1998
227'.92077—dc21   98-43494
                                            CIP

A WORD
FROM THE PUBLISHER

Years ago a movement was begun with the dream of uniting all Christians on the basis of a common purpose (world evangelism) under a common authority (The Word of God). The College Press NIV Commentary Series is a serious effort to join the scholarship of two branches of this unity movement so as to speak with one voice concerning the Word of God. Our desire is to provide a resource for your study of the New Testament that will benefit you whether you are preparing a Bible School lesson, a sermon, a college course or your own personal devotions. Today as we survey the wreckage of a broken world, we must turn again to the Lord and his Word, unite under his banner and communicate the life-giving message to those who are in desperate need. This is our purpose.

ACKNOWLEDGEMENTS

We want to thank College Press for the opportunity to write this commentary. We also want to thank those who read the manuscripts or sections thereof for their help. Allen thanks his colleagues Rick Oster and John Mark Hicks for their advice concerning 1 Peter. Mark thanks his colleague Gary Holloway and his student assistant Eric Simon.

We both thank our wives and daughters for patience while we took time away for another book.

We also thank Bob and Peggy Black. We and our sister Ginne owe so much to the wonderful Christian home in which they raised us. Our father was a great man of God, faithfully serving churches in Alabama and Georgia as an elder and Bible teacher. Our mother, who survives him, is a model of Christian womanhood and motherhood. The best parts of our life goals and achievements have their roots in their loving, Christian parenthood.

ABBREVIATIONS

BAGD..................*A Greek-English Lexicon of the New Testament by Bauer, Arndt, Gingrich, and Danker*

KJV....................*King James Version*

NASB..................*New American Standard Bible*

NIV....................*New International Version*

NRSV ....*New Revised Standard Version*

UBS[4]..................*United Bible Society Greek New Testament, 4th Edition*

THE BOOK OF
1 PETER

Allen Black

INTRODUCTION

This commentary is written for the general reader with a serious interest in Scripture. Its purpose is to provide a historical interpretation of 1 Peter; that is, an interpretation of what Peter meant to say to his ancient audience. I write with the conviction that modern readers can only determine God's message to us after and on the basis of a determination of Peter's message to his ancient contemporaries. Because I believe God worked through Peter and inspired his work, I believe it has great relevance to every reader in every age. But we can only determine what it means to us if we have first determined what it meant when Peter wrote it. It is this latter task that is the focus of most commentaries, including this one. I will occasionally make comments about what a given passage means today, but not consistently. I will consistently comment on what Peter meant to say to his original readers. I hope and pray that my readers will recognize the contemporary relevance of Peter's letter, even though it will not be my purpose to point it out or illustrate it. My purpose is to provide a base to build on for contemporary application.

I have been especially influenced by the commentaries by Paul Achtemeier and Ramsey Michaels.[1] I have also frequently consulted the commentaries by Leonard Goppelt and Peter Davids.[2] I often refer the reader to these works for further

---

[1]Paul J. Achtemeier, *1 Peter*, Hermeneia (Minneapolis: Fortress Press, 1996); J. Ramsey Michaels, *1 Peter*, Word Biblical Commentary, vol. 49 (Waco, TX: Word, 1988).

[2]Leonard Goppelt, *A Commentary on 1 Peter*, ed. Ferdinand Hahn, trans. and aug. John E. Alsup (Grand Rapids: Eerdmans, 1993); Peter H. Davids,

information, and even where I do not, the reader would be well advised to consult them for a scholar's depth of treatment.

I have commented on the NIV text. In some places where it seems deficient, I have provided an alternative translation, usually from the NRSV. The commentary makes note of the most significant textual variants and my opinions concerning them, but does not provide a list of manuscripts, versions, or church fathers. Interested readers should use the United Bible Societies' *Greek New Testament*.[3]

AUTHOR

Peter identifies himself in the opening words of the letter: "Peter, an apostle of Jesus Christ." The book clearly claims to have been written by the well-known apostle, a leading figure in the Gospels and in the first half of the book of Acts.

This claim is well supported by second century evidence. Some even argue that 1 Clement, written near the end of the first century, reflects use of 1 Peter.[4] It is certainly true that Polycarp of Smyrna knew and used 1 Peter. This is repeatedly reflected in his letter to the Philippians, written in the first half of the second century.[5] It is all the more significant since Smyrna was in one of the regions Peter addressed.

This is also true of Hierapolis, the home of Papias, who also wrote in the first half of the second century. According

---

The First Epistle of Peter, New International Commentary on the New Testament (Grand Rapids: Eerdmans, 1990).

[3]Barbara and Kurt Aland, et al., ed., *The Greek New Testament*, 4th rev. ed. (United Bible Societies, 1993). See also the discussions in Bruce M. Metzger, *A Textual Commentary on the Greek New Testament*, 2nd ed. (United Bible Societies, 1994).

[4]See the citations in Michaels, *1 Peter*, p. xxxiii, although he states that the common elements in 1 Peter and 1 Clement do not qualify "as hard evidence for literary dependence."

[5]Ibid., p. xxxii.

to Eusebius, Papias used quotations from the first epistle of Peter.[6]

In the latter part of the second century Irenaeus cited 1 Peter and explicitly mentioned Peter as the author.[7] All subsequent ancient Christian authors agree.[8]

The only evidence that some believe might indicate another opinion is that the Muratorian Canon (late second century) does not list 1 Peter. Others believe that 1 Peter was originally listed and is omitted because of the corrupt state of our copy of this list.[9] In any case it would be a questionable argument from silence to use the omission as evidence that the author of the Canon knew 1 Peter and considered it to be falsely ascribed. He was quite capable of identifying works which he considered to be falsely ascribed.[10]

Until modern times Peter's authorship of 1 Peter was universally accepted among Christians. However, many modern scholars, including Goppelt and Achtemeier, consider the book pseudepigraphical.[11] Their arguments are not compelling.

One argument against Petrine authorship is the good quality of the Greek in 1 Peter. However, in recent decades there has been a growing awareness that Greek was widely used as a second language in Palestine. It is not improbable that, even without a special gift from the Spirit, Peter would have known Greek. Furthermore, 1 Peter 5:12 may indicate that Silvanus assisted Peter as his secretary. This is a debated point which is

---

[6]Eusebius *Ecclesiastical History* 3.39.17: "The same writer (Papias) used quotations from the first Epistle of John, and likewise also from that of Peter . . ." Eusebius wrote in the early fourth century.

[7]E.g., Irenaeus *Against Heresies* 4.9.2: "Peter says in his epistle."

[8]E.g., Tertullian and Origen. Cf. Michaels, *1 Peter*, p. xxxiii.

[9]Michaels, *1 Peter*, pp. xxxiii-xxxiv.

[10]Concerning two such works he says, "There is said to be another letter in Paul's name to the Laodiceans, and another to the Alexandrines, [both] forged in accordance with Marcion's heresy . . ." See the full text in F.F. Bruce, *The Canon of Scripture* (Downers Grove, IL: InterVarsity, 1988), pp. 159-161.

[11]Goppelt, *1 Peter*, pp. 48-50; Achtemeier, *1 Peter*, pp. 1-43.

discussed in the comments on that verse. But if Silvanus did secretarial work for Peter, then he may have influenced the Greek style.

A second argument used against Peter having written 1 Peter is the similarity of the content of parts of 1 Peter to the letters of Paul. However, such similarities are not surprising. The incident Paul recounts in Galatians 2 does not indicate that he and Peter remained at odds with each other or that they did not share many common emphases.

A third argument is that the references to persecution indicate a late date, perhaps during the reign of Domitian (A.D. 81-96) or Trajan (A.D. 98-117) — after the death of Peter during the reign of Nero (A.D. 54-68). However, there are no clear indications of state-ordered persecution in 1 Peter. Fortunately, this argument has lost much of its force because most contemporary scholars agree that the persecution reflected in 1 Peter does not presuppose a government-sponsored persecution.

In the light of the weakness of arguments to the contrary and the strength of the second century support for Peter as the author, the claim made in 1 Peter 1:1 should be accepted. The author is Peter the apostle.

PLACE OF COMPOSITION

First Peter 5:13 says "She who is in Babylon, chosen together with you, sends you her greetings, and so does my son Mark." Peter was in "Babylon." There are three possible referents: Mesopotamian Babylon, a Roman military settlement named Babylon (located near modern Cairo, Egypt), and the city of Rome. The most likely choice is Rome. Rome is symbolically designated "Babylon" in the book of Revelation and several Jewish works (including 4 Ezra and 2 Baruch). One weakness of this approach is that 1 Peter appears to be the earliest such reference.

But there is reasonably good evidence that Peter went to Rome. Clement of Rome, writing in the mid-90s, implies that Peter and Paul were martyred in Rome during the Neronian persecution brought on by the fire in Rome in July of A.D. 64.[12] In the early second century Ignatius's letter to the Romans seems to assume that Peter had been in Rome.[13] Beginning in the second half of the second century there is a steady stream of references to Peter in Rome (although many of them are mixed in with dubious assertions about Peter founding the Roman church).[14]

In addition to Peter, 1 Peter 5:13 places Mark in "Babylon" as well. If Colossians and Philemon were written from Rome, they place Mark there with Paul (Col 4:10; Phlm 24).

DATE

The previous paragraph points out that 1 Clement 5-6 suggests that Peter died in the Neronian persecution. As in the case of Peter's presence in Rome, sources from the late second century and beyond provide a steady stream of references to Peter's martyrdom under Nero (mixed with various dubious claims).[15] The vast majority of scholars accept the idea that Peter was martyred by order of Nero between A.D. 64 and 68.[16] Since Peter is the author, 1 Peter must have been written no later than A.D. 68.

Few, if any, would suggest a date earlier than the 60s. Earlier dates might not allow adequate time for Peter to come to Rome or for Christianity to spread through most of Asia Minor.

---

[12]1 Clement 5-6.

[13]Ignatius *Romans* 4.3, "I do not give you orders like Peter and Paul . . ."

[14]See the overview in Jack Finegan, *Handbook of Biblical Chronology*, rev. ed. (Peabody, MA: Hendrickson, 1998), pp. 374-389.

[15]Ibid.

[16]For the contrary view see Michaels, *1 Peter*, pp. lvii-lxi.

RECIPIENTS

Concerning the five provinces listed in 1 Peter 1:1 see the commentary for details. They encompass most of Asia Minor (modern Turkey). Peter addressed Christians who were scattered throughout these areas.

The fact that Peter addressed his readers with the term "Diaspora" or "Dispersion" (1:1) misled many in the past to maintain that his readers were primarily *Jewish* Christians. The term "Diaspora," meaning "scattered," was used frequently by the Jews to refer to those who had been scattered throughout the world, away from their Palestinian homeland. However, there is a consensus among modern interpreters that Peter used it metaphorically to include Gentile Christians.[17] All Christians live away from their homeland with God.

Besides the likelihood that many Gentiles had become Christians in these predominantly Gentile regions, several verses in 1 Peter indicate that many of the readers came out of a pagan past. See, for example, 1:14, "do not conform to the evil desires you had when you lived in ignorance"; 1:18, "you were redeemed from the evil way of life handed down to you from your forefathers"; and 4:3, "you have spent enough time in the past doing what pagans choose to do."

ENCOURAGING THE PERSECUTED

First Peter 5:12 sums up Peter's purpose: "I have written to you briefly, encouraging you and testifying that this is the true grace of God. Stand fast in it." Peter's letter was a word of encouragement to Christians who were facing persecution and needed encouragement to stand firm in their faith.

---

[17]Achtemeier, *1 Peter*, pp. 50-51.

Earlier interpreters often thought of these persecutions as state-sponsored persecutions leading to imprisonment and death. More recent interpreters have noticed that the nature and extent of the persecutions is not very specific.[18] The only specific reference to physical persecution is the reference in 2:20 to Christian slaves being beaten. There is no reference to state-sponsored persecution.

But that the persecutions were severe is clear from such references as 1:6, "You may have had to suffer grief in all kinds of trials" and 4:12, "do not be surprised at the painful trial you are suffering."

We are familiar with the antagonistic environment the early Christians lived in from reading Acts and Paul's letters. In the early second century several pagan writers provide further evidence of how Christians were perceived by others. In writing about Nero's persecution of Christians Tacitus describes them as "a class hated for their abominations" and calls Christianity "a deadly superstition . . . hideous and shameful." In describing the same event Suetonius describes Christians as "a class of men given to a new and wicked superstition." During roughly the same period of time Pliny, the Roman governor of Bithynia (one of the five regions Peter addressed), wrote to the emperor Trajan and described Christianity as "a perverse and extravagant superstition."[19] These are the kinds of criticisms Peter presumably had in mind when he made comments like "they accuse you of doing wrong" (2:12) and they "speak maliciously against your good behavior in Christ" (3:16).

Peter wrote to remind these readers of what God had done for them in Christ (e.g., 1:1-12; 2:4-10) and to encourage them to stand firm (e.g., 1:13-25; 2:11-25). We can benefit from overhearing what he said.

---

[18]Ibid., pp. 28-36.

[19]For translations and discussions of all three texts see Everett Ferguson, *Backgrounds of Early Christianity*, 2nd ed. (Grand Rapids: Eerdmans, 1993), pp. 556-559.

OUTLINE

I. THE GREETING — 1:1-2

II. A CALL TO BE HOLY — 1:3–2:10
   A. The Hope of Salvation — 1:3-9
   B. The Glory of This Salvation — 1:10-12
   C. Be Holy in All You Do — 1:13-16
   D. Live in Reverent Fear as Those Redeemed by Christ's Blood — 1:17-21
   E. Love One Another as Those Born Again through the Word of God — 1:22-25
   F. Crave Pure Spiritual Milk — 2:1-3
   G. God's Chosen People through Jesus — 2:4-10

III. INSTRUCTIONS FOR EXEMPLARY LIVING IN SOCIETY'S STRUCTURES — 2:11–3:12
   A. Live Good Lives among the Pagans — 2:11-12
   B. Submit to the Governing Authorities — 2:13-17
   C. Slaves, Submit to Your Masters — 2:18-25
      1. Submit Even to Harsh Masters — 2:18-20
      2. Follow the Example of Christ — 2:21-25
   D. Wives, Submit to Your Husbands — 3:1-6
   E. Husbands, Be Considerate — 3:7
   F. General Instructions for All — 3:8-12

IV. ENCOURAGEMENT TO THOSE WHO SUFFER FOR DOING GOOD — 3:13–4:11
   A. Do Not Be Frightened — 3:13-17
   B. Christ Also Suffered — And Was Exalted — 3:18-22

    C. Live for the Will of God — 4:1-6

    D. Love and Serve Each Other — 4:7-11

  V. MORE EXHORTATIONS TO BE STEADFAST
    IN THE FACE OF SUFFERING — 4:12–5:11

    A. Rejoice When You Suffer for Christ — 4:12-19

    B. Show Humility in Your Relationships,
    Especially You Who Shepherd — 5:1-5

    C. A Summarizing Call to Suffer for Christ — 5:6-11

VI. CONCLUDING REMARKS — 5:12-14

BIBLIOGRAPHY

Achtemeier, Paul J. *1 Peter*. Hermeneia. Minneapolis: Fortress Press, 1996.

Aland, Barbara, Kurt Aland, et al., eds. *The Greek New Testament*. 4th Rev. Ed. United Bible Societies, 1993.

Bauer, Walter. *A Greek-English Lexicon of the New Testament and Other Early Christian Literature*. 2d Ed. Rev. William F. Arndt, F. Wilbur Gingrich, and Frederick W. Danker. Chicago: University of Chicago Press, 1979.

Bigg, Charles. *Epistles of St. Peter and St. Jude*. International Critical Commentary. Edinburgh: T & T Clark, 1901.

Bruce, F.F. *The Canon of Scripture*. Downers Grove, IL: InterVarsity, 1988.

Carson, D.A., D.J. Moo, and L. Morris. *An Introduction to the New Testament*. Grand Rapids: Zondervan, 1992.

Dalton, W.J. *Christ's Proclamation to the Spirits: A Study of 1 Peter 3:18–4:6*. 2nd Ed. Analecta Biblica 23. Rome: Pontifical Biblical Institute, 1989.

Davids, Peter H. *The First Epistle of Peter*. New International Commentary on the New Testament. Grand Rapids: Eerdmans, 1990.

Elliott, J.H. *The Elect and the Holy: An Exegetical Examination of 1 Peter 2:4-10 and the Phrase βασίλειον ἱεράτευμα*. Novum Testamentum. Supplement 12. Leiden: Brill, 1966.

Ferguson, Everett. *Backgrounds of Early Christianity.* 2nd Ed. Grand Rapids: Eerdmans, 1993.

Finegan, Jack. *Handbook of Biblical Chronology.* Rev. ed. Peabody, MA: Hendrickson, 1998.

France, R.T. "Exegesis in Practice: Two Samples." In *New Testament Exegesis.* Ed. I. Howard Marshall. Grand Rapids: Eerdmans, 1977.

Goppelt, Leonard. *A Commentary on 1 Peter.* Ed. Ferdinand Hahn. Trans. and Aug. John E. Alsup. Grand Rapids: Eerdmans, 1993.

Grudem, Wayne. *The First Epistle of Peter.* Tyndale New Testament Commentaries. Grand Rapids: Eerdmans, 1988.

Hemer, Colin. "The Address of 1 Peter." *Expository Times* 89 (1977-78): 239-243.

Hort, F.J.A. *The First Epistle of St. Peter 1:1–2:17.* London: Macmillan, 1898.

Jones, R.B. "Christian Behavior under Fire (First Epistle of Peter)." *Review and Expositor* 46 (1949): 56-66.

Kelly, J.N.D. *A Commentary on the Epistles of Peter and of Jude.* Harper New Testament Commentary. New York: Harper and Row, 1969.

Marshall, I. Howard. *1 Peter.* IVP New Testament Commentary Series. Downers Grove, IL: InterVarsity, 1991.

Metzger, Bruce M. *A Textual Commentary on the Greek New Testament.* 2nd Ed. United Bible Societies, 1994.

Michaels, J. Ramsey. *1 Peter.* Word Biblical Commentary. Vol. 49. Waco, TX: Word, 1988.

Moffatt, James. *The General Epistles.* The Moffatt New Testament Commentary. New York: Harper and Brothers, 1940.

O'Brien, P.T. "Letters, Letter Forms." In *Dictionary of Paul and His Letters.* Eds. G.F. Hawthorne, R.P. Martin, and D.G. Reid. 550-553. Downers Grove, IL: InterVarsity, 1993.

Osburn, Carroll D., ed. *Essays on Women in Earliest Christianity.* 2 Vols. Joplin, MO: College Press, 1993, 1995.

Piper, John and Wayne Grudem, eds. *Recovering Biblical Manhood and Womanhood: A Response to Evangelical Feminism.* Wheaton, IL: Crossway, 1991.

Selwyn, E.G. *The First Epistle of St. Peter.* London: Macmillan, 1946.

Wallace, Daniel B. *Greek Grammar beyond the Basics.* Grand Rapids: Zondervan, 1996.

1 PETER 1

I. THE GREETING (1:1-2)

¹Peter, an apostle of Jesus Christ,

To God's elect, strangers in the world, scattered throughout Pontus, Galatia, Cappadocia, Asia and Bithynia, ²who have been chosen according to the foreknowledge of God the Father, through the sanctifying work of the Spirit, for obedience to Jesus Christ and sprinkling by his blood:

Grace and peace be yours in abundance.

Peter begins his letter with a Christian adaptation of the common style of Greek letters in his day.[1] Most letters began with "X (the sender) to Y (the recipient), greeting." Peter adds Christian descriptions of himself and his recipients, and he replaces the word "greeting" with a Christian adaptation. Similar Christian adaptations of the opening of letters are well-known through the writings of the apostle Paul. Compare also the openings of 2 Peter, 2-3 John, and Jude.

The descriptive phrases that make up most of this greeting are not just ornamental. They introduce themes that will be important for the letter as a whole. By the end of the first two verses Peter has established his authority, reminded his readers of their election and sanctification, framed his readers' lives with the metaphor of living as strangers in this world, and summoned them to obedience.

---

[1]See D.A. Carson, D.J. Moo, and L. Morris, *An Introduction to the New Testament* (Grand Rapids: Zondervan, 1992), pp. 231-233.

1:1 Peter, an apostle of Jesus Christ,

Peter is the Greek translation of the Aramaic word Cephas, a name given to Simon by Jesus (Matt 16:18). Peter, like Cephas, means "rock."[2] We have no evidence that it was used as a personal name before Jesus used it for Simon.[3]

Peter's identification of himself as "an apostle" is similar to the opening words of nine of Paul's letters. Second Peter also opens with a reference to Peter's apostleship. In many of Paul's letters and in 2 Peter, this opening claim seems to have a defensive nuance in light of the letter's subsequent indications that the author's authority was disputed by some. First Peter shows no signs of Peter's needing to defend himself to his audience. Nevertheless, the term apostle is no doubt used to highlight his apostolic authority.

To God's elect,

The Greek text does not include the word "God's," but the translation is a fair one since the clear implication is that God did the choosing.[4] The word Peter uses has a rich biblical heritage. The Jews found their identity and the basis of their lives in the fact that they were God's chosen people (see, e.g., Deut 7:6-8). The New Testament frequently identifies Christians as elect or chosen. In 1 Peter 2:9 Peter will identify Christians as "a chosen people," using the same word ἐκλεκτός (eklektos) here translated "elect." The same word is also used of Christ in 2:4 and 6 (where it is translated "chosen"). Christians are

---

[2]Walter Bauer, *A Greek-English Lexicon of the New Testament and Other Early Christian Literature*, 2d ed., rev. William F. Arndt, F. Wilbur Gingrich, and Frederick W. Danker (Chicago: University of Chicago Press, 1979), p. 654. Hereafter cited as *BAGD*.

[3]Ibid. The Greek word for rock was a feminine noun. Peter is a masculine noun. There was a similar masculine name known before Jesus' time, but it had a different ending. Our Peter is Πέτρος (*Petros*), the known name was Πέτρων (*Petrōn*).

[4]Cf. 1 Peter 2:4, where Jesus is described as "chosen" with the explicit modifier "by God."

chosen or elect through the chosen or elect One, Jesus Christ. The idea that Christians are God's chosen people is fundamental to Peter's thinking, as is apparent in 1:13–2:10. Peter is already laying the foundation for his appeals to these Christians to live up to their holy calling.

strangers in the world,

This phrase translates παρεπίδημος (*parepidēmos*), the second word Peter uses to describe his audience. Although this word is not a common description of Christians like the word "elect," it is found outside of 1 Peter in Hebrews 11:13. Peter uses it again in 1 Peter 2:11. Translated "exiles" by the NRSV, it refers to people who live outside of their homeland, whether by force or by preference.[5] The translation "strangers in the world" rightly indicates that Peter is not thinking of his audience as literally aliens whose homeland is outside of Asia Minor, but rather is using the term metaphorically. The writer of Hebrews explains the idea: "They [the Old Testament patriarchs] confessed they were strangers and foreigners on the earth . . . they desire a better country, that is, a heavenly one" (Heb 11:13-16, NRSV). Paul uses the same basic idea in Philippians 3:20: "But our citizenship is in heaven." The idea that Christians are citizens of heaven and live as foreigners on the earth is an important concept that Peter will build upon.

scattered

By using "exiles" for the previous word, the NRSV is able to translate this term more precisely as "Dispersion." Peter's addressees are "exiles of the Dispersion." The term "Dispersion" or "Diaspora" was a technical term with a long heritage among the Jews. It referred to the Jews who were scattered or dispersed from their homeland Israel into the various

---

[5]Achtemeier, *1 Peter*, p. 81.

countries of the world. It is used in this literal sense in John 7:35.[6] However, 1 Peter 1:1 and James 1:1 use it metaphorically for Christians. In 1 Peter it is closely related to the term translated "strangers in the world."[7] Christians are part of a metaphorical "Diaspora." They live away from their true homeland, heaven.

As discussed in the Introduction to this commentary, some interpreters, especially in the past, have taken this term to mean that Peter specifically addresses Jewish Christians, since only Jews would be part of the literal Diaspora. However, several verses (e.g., 4:3-4) indicate that Peter's audience includes Gentile Christians. Most contemporary interpreters rightly take this term in a metaphorical sense. It is important for modern readers to understand this and to see that we, too, are "exiles of the Dispersion."

throughout Pontus, Galatia, Cappadocia, Asia and Bithynia,

These five regions cover the majority of ancient Asia Minor (modern Turkey). Three of them — Pontus, Cappadocia, and Asia — are listed in Acts 2:9 as the homelands of some of those who heard Peter preach on the day of Pentecost. This may provide a clue to how these churches originated. We have no knowledge of Peter traveling in these regions, and it is in any event unlikely that he had covered much of this area of some 300,000 square miles.[8]

The most popular hypothesis concerning the order of these provinces is the suggestion of Hort that it was determined by the probable route of a letter carrier, who began at a port on the Black Sea and circled clockwise through the regions.[9]

---

[6]"The Jews said to one another, 'Where does this man intend to go that we will not find him? Does he intend to go to the Dispersion among the Greeks . . .?'" (NRSV)

[7]The Greek word is in the genitive case and modifies "exile," as the NRSV translation indicates.

[8]Mileage estimate from Michaels, *1 Peter*, p. 4.

[9]F.J.A. Hort, *The First Epistle of St. Peter 1:1–2:17* (London: Macmillan,

1:2 who have been chosen according to the foreknowledge of God the Father,

"Who have been chosen" is a second translation of the very same word previously translated "God's elect." Although the Greek word appears only in verse 1, the NIV repeats it in verse 2 to preserve its link to the phrase "according to the foreknowledge of God."

The idea is not only that God knew in advance that there would be a chosen people, but more specifically that he purposed in advance to bring them into being. This is suggested by the parallel in 1 Peter 1:20, which uses the verb form of the word "foreknowledge" to speak of Christ as "chosen (= foreknown) before the creation of the world." God did not only fore-see that he would send Christ, but he fore-planned it. That very plan entailed a plan to create a people around Christ. His "fore-knowledge" involved "fore-planning" or "fore-purposing." The predestination spoken of here is a corporate predestining of a people called into being by their response to Christ. God foreknew that he would send Christ and save those who accepted him.

The term Father will be especially important later (see verse 17).

through the sanctifying work of the Spirit,

This phrase indicates the means by which the election of Christians occurs: they are set apart by the Spirit. The idea that the Holy Spirit sanctifies or sets people apart as God's people is a common New Testament idea. Second Thessalonians 2:13 provides a nice parallel to Peter's combination of election and sanctification: "from the beginning God chose you to be saved through the sanctifying work of the Spirit . . ."

The concept of sanctification can be understood by comparing the sanctification of people to the sanctification of the

---

1898), pp. 157-184. See also Colin Hemer, "The Address of 1 Peter," *Expository Times* 89 (1977-78): 239-243.

temple or its utensils. A sanctified building, lampstand, or pot is designated to be used only in service to God. A sanctified person has also been set apart for service. The Holy Spirit both marks us for God's service and empowers us to render that service.

for obedience to Jesus Christ and sprinkling by his blood:
The key phrases in verse 2 relate back to the word "chosen" (or "elect"): Christians are chosen according to the foreknowledge of God, chosen through the sanctifying work of the Spirit, chosen to be obedient, and chosen to be sprinkled with the blood of Jesus.

The people whom God chose and set apart are to be obedient. This will be a major theme of Peter's letter, which repeatedly reminds the readers of what God has done for them and then summons obedience on that basis.

The phrase "sprinkling by his blood" reflects the language and ideas of Exodus 24:7-8: "Then he [Moses] took the Book of the Covenant and read it to the people. They responded, 'We will do everything the LORD has said; we will obey.' Moses then took the blood, sprinkled it on the people and said, 'This is the blood of the covenant that the LORD has made with you in accordance with all these words.'" In this text, which portrays the ratification of God's covenant with Israel, the people declare their commitment to obedience and then Moses sprinkles sacrificial blood on them to ratify their covenant. Peter also refers to obedience and the sprinkling of blood. He probably chose this unusual language to remind them that they are God's covenant people. Their covenant is ratified by the sprinkling of blood more precious than that of bulls and goats, the blood of Christ (compare the use of Exodus 24 in Heb 9:13-22).

Grace and peace be yours in abundance.
At this point in the typical Greek letter the sender used the word "greeting" — in Greek χαίρειν (*chairein*). Paul and

Peter substituted the word "grace" — in Greek χάρις (*charis* — note the similarity to *chairein*). "Grace and peace be yours in abundance" is an adaptation of the usual style, similar to various Christian substitutions for the word "sincerely" near the end of modern letters. Peter's version, using the verb translated "be yours in abundance" (see also 2 Pet 1:2 and Jude 2), is slightly different from Paul's.[10]

Adaptations of common letter forms tend to have more meaning than simple repetition. The content of the letter will show that Peter believes his readers truly need God's grace and peace.

II. A CALL TO BE HOLY (1:3–2:10)

A. THE HOPE OF SALVATION (1:3-9)

[3]Praise be to the God and Father of our Lord Jesus Christ! In his great mercy he has given us new birth into a living hope through the resurrection of Jesus Christ from the dead, [4]and into an inheritance that can never perish, spoil or fade — kept in heaven for you, [5]who through faith are shielded by God's power until the coming of the salvation that is ready to be revealed in the last time. [6]In this you greatly rejoice, though now for a little while you may have had to suffer grief in all kinds of trials. [7]These have come so that your faith — of greater worth than gold, which perishes even though refined by fire — may be proved genuine and may result in praise, glory and honor when Jesus Christ is revealed. [8]Though you have not seen him, you love him; and even though you do not see him now, you believe in him and

---

[10]It is most similar to Theodotion's Greek version of Daniel 4:1 and 6:26 ("Peace be yours in abundance"). Early Christian adaptations of the Greek greeting probably had precedents in previous Jewish adaptations. See Achtemeier, *1 Peter*, pp. 79-80.

**are filled with an inexpressible and glorious joy, [9]for you are
receiving the goal of your faith, the salvation of your souls.**

In some Greek letters the next item following the greeting
is a sentence referring to the writer's prayer to a god (or the
gods) on behalf of the health or welfare of the recipient.[11]
Paul adapted this part of the letter form into a significant
item in most of his letters. He describes his thanksgiving to
God and his petitions to God in ways that often introduce
major themes of the rest of the letter.[12] Similarly, Peter's
opening praise to God is such a basic part of the letter that
most interpreters even consider it to be the beginning of the
body of the letter. First Peter 1:3-12 reminds the readers of
the great hope of salvation that they have received and thus
lays the foundation for the appeals that begin in verse 13.

1:3 Praise be to the God and Father of our Lord Jesus Christ!
Verses 3-5 are the heart of the section encompassing verses 3-12. They describe the great hope of salvation that God
has provided. Verses 6-9 then encourage the readers to persevere in trials by keeping this hope in mind. And verses 10-12
reemphasize its great value.

As Peter begins to describe the hope of salvation he bursts
forth in praise. The exact statement "Praise be to [or blessed
be] the God and Father of our Lord Jesus Christ" is also
found in 2 Corinthians 1:3 and Ephesians 1:3. In all three
cases it introduces a recounting of God's blessings.

In his great mercy he has given us new birth into a living hope
God's great mercy has been demonstrated by our new
birth into a living hope. Peter's use of the new birth imagery

---

[11]P.T. O'Brien, "Letters, Letter Forms," in *Dictionary of Paul and His
Letters*, eds. G.F. Hawthorne, R.P. Martin, and D.G. Reid (Downers Grove,
IL: InterVarsity, 1993), p. 551.

[12]Ibid.

is illuminated by 1 Peter 1:23 and 2:2. The seed which begets us to a new birth is the word of God (1:23; cf. 1:25). The result is that we become like newborn infants (2:2). The image of a new birth is also found elsewhere in the New Testament as a metaphor for what happens when one becomes a Christian (John 3:5; Titus 3:5).

The focus of the sentence found in verses 3-5 is the "living hope," which is further described in verse 4 as an inheritance and in verse 5 as the coming salvation. It is the hope of eternal salvation. By describing it as "living" Peter means that it is not vain or foolish, an idle wish. Like the "living and enduring word of God" the Christian's hope is based on something that "stands forever" (cf. vv. 23-25) and will not fade away (cf. v. 4). It is a foundation on which one can build a life.

through the resurrection of Jesus Christ from the dead,

God gave us new birth to this living hope through the resurrection of Jesus from the dead. As Paul put it, "If Christ has not been raised, our preaching is useless and so is your faith. . . . But Christ has indeed been raised from the dead, the first fruits of those who have fallen asleep. . . . Thanks be to God! He gives us the victory through our Lord Jesus Christ" (1 Cor 15:14,20,57). Christ's resurrection assures our eventual victory over death. It is the basis of our living hope.

1:4 and into an inheritance that can never perish, spoil or fade — kept in heaven for you,

The living hope of Christians is further defined as an inheritance. Christians, as children of God, receive an inheritance from him. The comparison of salvation to an inheritance is also found in Acts 20:32; Galatians 3:18; Colossians 3:24; Ephesians 1:14,18. Even in the Old Testament, the concept of an inheritance is (on rare occasion) used for one's eternal reward (e.g., Dan 12:13: "at the end of the days you will rise to receive your allotted inheritance"). The New Testament picks up on this usage.

Our inheritance is "imperishable, undefiled, and unfading" (NRSV translation). In Greek these three adjectives have a high degree of alliteration.[13] They emphasize that the inheritance Christians await is not subject to doubt. It is eternal. It is being kept in heaven by God himself.

Peter is prone to contrast the perishable with the imperishable. In verse 18 perishable things like gold and silver are set in contrast to the precious blood of Christ. In verses 23-25 he observes that all men perish, but the word of God is imperishable. In 3:3-4 he says women should not adorn themselves with fine clothing, braided hair, and jewels (things that perish), but with the imperishable beauty of a gentle and quiet spirit.

1:5 who through faith are shielded by God's power

The inheritance is not the only thing God is watching over. While he "keeps" our inheritance, he "shields" or "protects" (NRSV) us until we receive it. The word translated "shield" has military overtones. The idea of God "shielding" his people is common in the Old Testament (e.g., Gen 15:1; Ps 115:9-11). God is using his power to guard Christians until they receive their inheritance. Christians appropriate that protection through faith.

until the coming of the salvation that is ready to be revealed in the last time.

The "salvation that is ready to be revealed in the last time" is a more literal way of speaking of the "inheritance . . . kept in heaven." It is being kept in heaven now, but it will be revealed at the end of time. This salvation is the object of the Christian's living hope. Peter wants to focus his readers' attention on it in order to encourage them to persevere in their present circumstances.

---

[13]Ἄφθαρτον, ἀμίαντον, ἀμάραντον (*aphtharton, amianton, amaranton*).

1:6 In this you greatly rejoice,

The antecedent of "this" is not clear. In the Greek text the word "this" is either masculine or neuter, whereas the possible antecedents "hope," "inheritance," and "salvation" are all feminine. One could translate "in whom," treating God as the antecedent. The most common approach is to see the antecedent as the general content of the preceding two verses: that is, "in this" means in view of what has been said about the Christian's hope, inheritance, and salvation.[14]

In view of what they have to look forward to, Christians rejoice even when suffering. The verb "rejoice" (ἀγαλλιᾶσθε, *agalliasthe*) may be an imperative, as in the NRSV footnote, "Rejoice in this." Most translations and commentators treat it as an indicative, but in either case the sense of what is being said is not simply to describe Christian behavior, but to summon Christians to a certain behavior. Peter is providing a basis on which Christians can learn to deal with trials and even face them with rejoicing.

though now for a little while you may have had to suffer grief in all kinds of trials.

At this point we begin to learn about why Peter wrote. The Christians of Asia Minor had suffered, and Peter wrote to encourage them to steadfastness (cf. 5:12). As the letter progresses we will learn that in this particular case the various trials of these Christians are not from things like natural catastrophes or plagues, but were persecutions inflicted by their pagan neighbors. These Christians are specifically suffering for their faith and are under constant pressure to be unfaithful.

Peter has described the salvation they await as imperishable and unfading. By contrast their trials are "for a little

---

[14]Michaels, *1 Peter*, p. 27, takes the antecedent of "this" to be "the last time." This proposal may be correct since "the last time" is masculine and is the most immediate antecedent. The reason most reject this view is that it entails taking the present tense of "rejoice" as a "futuristic present": "in this [the last time] you *will* rejoice."

while." The idea is not that they only last a few days, months, or even years. "A little while" is in contrast to eternity. See 5:10, Romans 8:18, and especially 2 Corinthians 4:17 ("For our light and momentary troubles are achieving for us an eternal glory that far outweighs them all").

The trials that these Christians have endured have a notion of necessity: they "have *had* to suffer." Verse 7 seems to indicate that they "had" to suffer in order to prove their faith genuine. These sufferings, brought about by evil people, were allowed by God for a purpose.

1:7 These have come so that your faith — of greater worth than gold, which perishes even though refined by fire — may be proved genuine and may result in praise, glory and honor when Jesus Christ is revealed.

The persecutors intend these trials for evil, but God intends them for good (cf. Gen 50:20). The potential results of such trials are analogous to the process of refining gold. Gold ore is smelted in order to remove the impurities and expose the precious metal. Trials serve to refine the Christian and test his or her faithfulness. This analogy is common in the Old Testament: e.g., Psalm 66:10 ("For you, O God, tested us; you refined us like silver") and Zechariah 13:9 ("I [God] will refine them like silver and test them like gold").

Peter's use of the smelting analogy adds an emphasis on the importance of faithfulness. Gold, however valuable it may be, is a perishable commodity, doomed to perish with the earth. By contrast, genuine faith endures for eternity and results in praise, glory, and honor.

1:8 Though you have not seen him, you love him; and even though you do not see him now, you believe in him and are filled with an inexpressible and glorious joy,

This verse continues the themes of faith and joy in the face of suffering. Peter has just referred (v. 7) to the coming time of praise and glory and honor when they will see Jesus revealed. But at the present his readers have not seen and do not now see Jesus, and their current experience is one of suffering. Peter reminds them that even without sight Christians love and believe in Jesus and thus may be filled with joy. Peter would agree with Paul's comment that "We live by faith, not by sight" (2 Cor 5:7). He would also agree with Paul's statement before and after that one that nevertheless "we are always confident" (2 Cor 5:6,8). Although they had not seen him, the Christians of Asia Minor believed in and loved Jesus. They therefore could rejoice even now in the midst of their plight.

1:9 for you are receiving the goal of your faith, the salvation of your souls.

The context of verses 3-8 suggests strongly that the salvation here envisioned is the same as the inheritance kept in heaven (v. 4), the salvation ready to be revealed at the last time (v. 5), that which will happen when Jesus is revealed (v. 7). Nevertheless the verb "receive" (κομιζόμενοι, *komizomenoi*) is in the present tense. They are receiving this salvation now. How can this be true? Verse 8 provides an answer: they believe in what they do not see. Achtemeier rightly explains, "The sense is that Christians now obtain by faith what they will only fully enter into at the end . . ."[15] By faith they can rejoice even now.

The phrase "of your souls" is commonly misunderstood. The ancient Greeks and many modern Christians thought of the soul as a spiritual component separate from the body, which leaves the body at death. The ancient Jews and first century Christians thought more holistically about human beings and thought in terms of a resurrection of the whole person, including the body, which will then be transformed into a spiritual body (cf. 1 Cor 15). Peter's use of the word "soul" refers to the person, not a part of the person separable

---

[15]Achtemeier, *1 Peter*, p. 104.

from the body. See, for example, 1 Peter 3:20 where Peter says that in the ark eight "souls" were saved.[16]

B. THE GLORY OF THIS SALVATION (1:10-12)

[10]**Concerning this salvation, the prophets, who spoke of the grace that was to come to you, searched intently and with the greatest care, [11]trying to find out the time and circumstances to which the Spirit of Christ in them was pointing when he predicted the sufferings of Christ and the glories that would follow. [12]It was revealed to them that they were not serving themselves but you, when they spoke of the things that have now been told you by those who have preached the gospel to you by the Holy Spirit sent from heaven. Even angels long to look into these things.**

In verses 3-9 Peter called his readers' attention to the great hope of salvation which they had received and emphasized how this salvation was a cause for rejoicing even in the midst of suffering. In this next paragraph, verses 10-12, Peter continues to emphasize the hope of salvation. His primary goal in these verses is to highlight its greatness by observing that the ancient prophets and even angels longed to hear about this salvation which is now known to his readers.

1:10 Concerning this salvation, the prophets, who spoke of the grace that was to come to you, searched intently and with the greatest care,
According to Peter the living hope, the inheritance kept in heaven, the salvation which will be revealed when Jesus Christ is revealed — this salvation was of great interest to the ancient

---

[16]In this case the NIV omits the word "souls" altogether. The NRSV translates "eight persons." See also the NIV translation of 1 Peter 1:22 where the NIV (legitimately) uses "yourselves" for "your souls."

prophets of the Old Testament. It is commonplace in the New Testament to argue that the prophets spoke about the grace that would be revealed in Christ. Peter adds that they longed to know more.

Grace is a key concept in 1 Peter (as in all of the Bible). It first appears in the greeting "Grace and peace be yours in abundance" (v. 2). Most of its occurrences are to remind Peter's audience of what God has done for them through the gospel (1:10,13; 3:7; 5:10,12). At the end of the book, in his statement of purpose, he says he wants to encourage them to stand fast in "the true grace of God" (5:12).

1:11 trying to find out the time and circumstances to which the Spirit of Christ in them was pointing

There is some disagreement about how to render the Greek words here translated "the time and circumstances." The NRSV translates "the person or time." The arguments are technical[17] and the distinction is not of great importance. They wanted to know more details than they were given.

The phrase "Spirit of Christ" occurs here and in Romans 8:9. A similar phrase "Spirit of Jesus Christ" occurs in Philippians 1:19. In Romans 8:9 the Spirit of Christ seems to be equivalent to the Spirit of God and the Holy Spirit. This is probably Peter's intent, although it is possible to understand it to mean "the Spirit, namely, Christ." In this latter case Peter would be referring to Christ himself inspiring the prophets.[18]

when he predicted the sufferings of Christ and the glories that would follow.

What the Spirit led the prophets to speak of was the sufferings of Christ and the subsequent glories. That the prophets

---

[17]A decision revolves around whether the pronoun τίνα (*tina*) is masculine or neuter. Literally the possibilities are something like "whom or what sort of time" or "which [time] or what sort of time."

[18]So Achtemeier, *1 Peter*, p. 110.

spoke of the coming Messiah's suffering and death was
unheard of in pre-Christian Judaism, but a common understanding in early Christianity (see, e.g., Luke 24:25-26,44-45).
Luke 24:26 also says the prophets spoke about how the
Messiah would "then enter his glory." Peter's use of the plural
"glories" may refer to different phases of Jesus' being glorified: resurrection, ascension, enthronement with God, second
coming.[19] The prophets wanted to know more details about
these things.

This is the first reference in 1 Peter to the sufferings of
Christ. There will be several more. As Peter seeks to encourage these Christians to be faithful in the face of suffering, he
repeatedly reminds them of Christ's sufferings (1:18-19; 2:4,6-
8; 2:21-25; 3:18; 4:1,13; 5:1).

**1:12 It was revealed to them that they were not serving
themselves but you,**
The Spirit did not grant all the prophets' requests, reveal-
ing to them that these prophecies were not primarily for their
benefit but for those to come. Peter's readers are among the
privileged people whom the prophets served and who know
what the prophets longed to know.

**when they spoke of the things that have now been told you
by those who have preached the gospel to you by the Holy
Spirit sent from heaven.**
The things the prophets longed to know more about are
now made known in the preaching of the gospel. They
include the whole story of the sufferings, death, and subsequent glories of Christ. "By the Holy Spirit" underscores the
divine origin of the message of the gospel. The same Spirit
that inspired the prophets to predict these things now lies
behind the contemporary proclamation that they have happened. The divine origin of the message is highlighted by the

---

[19]Ibid., p. 111 n. 72.

divine origin of the Spirit who empowers it. He has been sent from heaven.

Even angels long to look into these things.

Peter's primary point here is clear: the salvation that Christians have heard about is so great that not only did the prophets long to hear more about it, but the angels also have an intense interest. Nevertheless, Peter's statement is tantalizingly brief. His choice of the present tense seems unexpected. Do the angels even now not know what human beings know? Does the present tense here actually refer to the angels' former longings? Does the translation "long to look" wrongly imply an unfulfilled longing? Selwyn is perhaps correct in suggesting that Peter speaks of the angels' intense interest, not their lack of knowledge. He cites Charles Wesley's lines: "Angels in fix'd amazement /Around our altars hover, /With eager gaze /Adore the grace /Of our Eternal Lover."[20]

C. BE HOLY IN ALL YOU DO (1:13-16)

[13]Therefore, prepare your minds for action; be self-controlled; set your hope fully on the grace to be given you when Jesus Christ is revealed. [14]As obedient children, do not conform to the evil desires you had when you lived in ignorance. [15]But just as he who called you is holy, so be holy in all you do; [16]for it is written: "Be holy, because I am holy."[a]

[a]*16* Lev. 11:44,45; 19:2; 20:7

Peter has focused his readers' attention on the hope of salvation which God has graciously provided through Christ. He has implicitly summoned them to face their trials with rejoicing. Now he turns to explicit imperatives. "Therefore" (διό,

---

[20]E.G. Selwyn, *The First Epistle of St. Peter* (London: Macmillan, 1946), pp. 138-139.

dio, v. 13), because they have such a great hope of salvation, they must live holy lives.

1:13 Therefore, prepare your minds for action;

"Prepare your minds for action" is literally, as in the NRSV footnote, "Gird up the loins of your mind." It is based upon the fact that in Peter's time the common attire was a garment that reached the ankle or knees and had to be tucked into the belt at the waist when engaged in physical labor.[21] In modern terms we might say "Roll up the shirt sleeves of your mind." In light of what God has done for us, we need to get serious about getting down to work for him.[22]

be self-controlled;

This exhortation is repeated in 4:7 and 5:8. The verb νήφω (*nēphō*) is similar to the English "be sober." Literally it means to refrain from drunkenness, but it was often (perhaps always in the New Testament) used in a figurative sense to refer to being "free from every form of mental and spiritual 'drunkenness', from excess, passion, rashness, confusion, etc.," that is, to be "well-balanced, self-controlled."[23] As verse 14 indicates, these Christians had once lived pagan lives following evil desires. Peter will later say they "have spent enough time in the past doing what pagans choose to do — living in debauchery, lust, drunkenness, orgies, carousing and detestable idolatry" (4:3). They now need self-control.

---

[21]Davids, *First Epistle*, p. 66.

[22]The first two verb forms in this verse are not imperatives, but participles. It is a debated point whether participles could serve as imperatives. See, e.g., Achtemeier, *1 Peter*, p. 117; and Daniel B. Wallace, *Greek Grammar beyond the Basics* (Grand Rapids: Zondervan, 1996), pp. 650-653. In 1:13 "prepare" and "be self-controlled" could be translated as participles, but they receive an imperatival connotation from their context and their dependence on the imperative verb translated "set your hope."

[23]*BAGD*, p. 538

set your hope fully on the grace to be given you when Jesus Christ is revealed.

Verses 3-12 have elaborated on "the grace to be given you when Jesus Christ is revealed." They await a glorious inheritance kept in heaven for them. They need to make that hope central to their lives and let it provide incentive for holy living. This is the second of three times Peter refers to "when Jesus Christ is revealed" (1:7,13; 4:13).

1:14 As obedient children, do not conform to the evil desires you had when you lived in ignorance.

This verse is the first of several verses that indicate Peter is addressing former pagans. The Bible frequently refers to Gentiles as those who are ignorant of God and his will (e.g., Gal 4:8-9; Eph 4:18). A later verse will specify some of the desires they used to guide their lives: lust, drunkenness, orgies, carousing, etc. (4:13). Now they must no longer live by their desires. They must live like obedient children. Peter has already twice spoken of God as our Father (1:2-3) and has observed that he "has given us a new birth." Christians must live as God's children and be obedient to their Father.

1:15 But just as he who called you is holy, so be holy in all you do; 1:16 for it is written: "Be holy, because I am holy."

These two verses crown Peter's exhortation with a familiar Old Testament theme. The verse cited in verse 16 could be any of several thematic verses in Leviticus (11:44-45; 19:2; 20:7,26), although Leviticus 19:2, part of the "Holiness Code" of Leviticus 17–26, is the most exact equivalent.[24] Like obedient children, Christians are to imitate their Father. The preceding verse, which defines the opposite of being holy as conforming to evil desires, indicates that Peter is focusing on the moral or spiritual aspects of being holy. Some aspects of

---

[24]See Michaels, *1 Peter*, p. 52 note d. There is a relatively insignificant variant involved in 1 Peter.

God's holiness, for example, qualities of deity such as his omnipotence, cannot be imitated by human beings. But his absolute purity of thought and action may and must be imitated, however pitiful our attempts may be. In a sense, every thought and behavior recommended by 1 Peter is a part of what it means to be holy (ἅγιος, *hagios*).

The call to holiness is a basic concept of 1 Peter, which has already surfaced in verse 2 ("the sanctifying [from the same Greek root] work of the Spirit"). It is prominent in the descriptions of Christians as a holy temple, a holy priesthood, and a holy people in 2:4-10. Christians are to live as persons dedicated to God's service.

The phrase "in all you do" paraphrases an expression that might be more literally translated "in all your way of life." The term "way of life" appears here for the first of several occurrences in Peter's writings: 1 Peter 1:18; 2:12; 3:1,2,16; 2 Peter 2:7; 3:11. Peter is particularly fond of this word, which occurs only five times in the rest of the New Testament. The Christian's "way of life" should be characterized by holiness (1:15; 2 Pet 3:11). Their former "way of life" was characterized by futility (1:18).

D. LIVE IN REVERENT FEAR AS THOSE REDEEMED BY CHRIST'S BLOOD (1:17-21)

[17]Since you call on a Father who judges each man's work impartially, live your lives as strangers here in reverent fear. [18]For you know that it was not with perishable things such a silver or gold that you were redeemed from the empty way of life handed down to you from your forefathers, [19]but with the precious blood of Christ, a lamb without blemish or defect. [20]He was chosen before the creation of the world, but was revealed in these last times for your sake. [21]Through him you believe in God, who raised him from the dead and glorified him, and so your faith and hope are in God.

Peter continues his appeal for a holy lifestyle. In 1:22–2:3 he will provide more specifics of what that entails. In the present paragraph he continues to motivate. He uses several motivations. Christians need to be holy because God will sit in judgment (v. 17). They need to remember their homeland in heaven and treat their current situation as a temporary sojourn in a foreign land (v. 17). They need to recognize that their inherited lifestyle was futile (v. 18). God is worthy of their trust, having raised Jesus from the dead (v. 21). And the key motivator of these verses is that they need to remember that they were redeemed from their empty way of life at tremendous cost, the death of Christ.

1:17 Since you call on a Father who judges each man's work impartially,

The God whom Christians call upon and turn to as their Father will sit in judgment over all the earth. His judgment will be based upon each person's actions and it will be impartial. The fact that Christians are God's children (cf. v. 14) is not an excuse for unfaithfulness.

The idea that God will judge each one according to his actions is a repeated biblical theme (e.g., Ps 62:12; Prov 24:12; Rom 2:6; Rev 22:12). By speaking of judgment based on each man's work, Peter does not intend to nullify grace, which he has already introduced and will turn back to almost immediately. His perspective may be understood by extending Peter's analogy of father and child. Obedient children are not perfect children, but they may expect grace for what they do wrong. Rebellious, disobedient children are another matter. Certain partial and biased fathers may tolerate rebellion, but the impartial father will not treat a rebellious child in the same way as an obedient one.

live your lives as strangers here in reverent fear.

Peter does not hesitate to use the motivation of fear of God's wrath (cf. 2:17; 3:2,15). It is difficult to describe the

precise nuance the word for "fear" (φόβος, *phobos*) ought to
have when one speaks of the fear of God that is appropriate
for the Christian. We do not want to overlook 1 John 4:18
"one who fears is not made perfect in love." But neither
should we overlook the many passages which use the same
Greek noun or verb to speak of appropriate Christian
responses to God (e.g., Acts 9:31; 2 Cor 7:1; Phil 2:12). The
NIV struggles with this issue in 1 Peter, translating the same
word "reverent fear" here, "reverence" in 3:2, and "respect"
in 3:15. Again the analogy of a parent-child relationship may
be helpful. There are appropriate and inappropriate senses in
which a child may fear a parent. The Christian should not live
in fear of condemnation, but should have confidence before
God. Nevertheless, we should live in what the NIV calls "reverent fear." Furthermore, we should realize that if we were to
turn back to the world, we would return to "a fearful expectation of judgment and of raging fire" (Heb 10:27).

The term for "stranger" which Peter introduces here differs from the term translated "strangers in the world" in
verse 1. It is, however, a similar term and both are juxta-
posed in 2:11. As we shall see at that point, Peter's juxtaposition may reflect Genesis 23:4 in which the Septuagint translation has Abraham use both terms to describe himself as an
alien among the Hittites: "I am an alien and a stranger
among you." To some extent the two terms were used with
somewhat different nuances. The term used in 1:1 could be
used for "sojourner," with connotations of a temporary stay.
The juxtaposition of both terms in 1 Peter 2:11 and the use
of the overlapping concept of the Dispersion in 1:1 suggest
that Peter was not interested in such distinctions, but simply
wanted to express the idea that Christians live upon the
earth as foreigners whose true citizenship is in heaven. Later
Christian adaptations of this idea have often used the term
"pilgrim."

1:18 For you know that it was not with perishable things such as silver or gold that you were redeemed

Of the various motivational themes introduced in this paragraph, the most central is the theme of redemption by the blood of Christ. The New Testament frequently portrays Jesus' death as a redemption, a practice Jesus himself began (Mark 10:45). In our context Peter contrasts the redemption bought with Christ's blood with common practices of redeeming persons or things by payment of money. Ransoms were paid to purchase freedom for prisoners of war. A purchase price could be paid to free a slave. The Septuagint uses the verb Peter uses to describe many redemptive purchases, including the redemption of property (e.g., Lev 25), redemption for a firstborn animal or child (Exod 13:12-13), and payment of the atonement price of one-half shekel per person (Exod 30:12-13). Michaels and others think a particular background that may have come to mind for Peter's audience is a practice of slave manumission in which the slave paid the ransom price to a local temple and when he was free from his master he was nevertheless enslaved to the god or goddess to whose temple he had given the ransom money.[25]

from the empty way of life handed down to you from your forefathers,

Here is another indication of the pagan background of Peter's addressees. Some of these futile ways are listed in 4:3: "debauchery, lust, drunkenness, orgies, carousing and detestable idolatry."

1:19 but with the precious blood of Christ, a lamb without blemish or defect.

Christians are redeemed by something much more valuable than gold or silver, the precious[26] blood of Christ. Peter

---

[25]Michaels, *1 Peter*, p. 64.

[26]The earliest commentary on "precious" is in the words of Clement in

has already mentioned the importance of Jesus' blood (v. 2). The New Testament emphasis on the blood of Jesus is rooted in the Old Testament emphasis on blood as the seat of life and on the importance of blood in sacrificial rites. That Peter has in mind the notion of sacrifice is further indicated by his description of Jesus as "a lamb without blemish or defect."

The reference to Jesus as a lamb causes some to think of the Passover.[27] Since the Passover event was a redemptive event for Israel this may be correct, but the Passover slaughter of the lambs was not in itself redemptive. We should probably think more generally of lambs used in the sacrificial system.[28]

The word ἄμωμος (amōmos) translated "without blemish" is used on many occasions in the Septuagint (e.g., Num 28:3,9) to indicate that God did not accept the sacrifice of an imperfect animal. The second term ("without defect") does not occur in the Septuagint, but simply reinforces the first term.

Peter's audience should leave their old empty way of life and live in reverent fear because they have been redeemed by the sacrifice of Christ.

1:20 He was chosen before the creation of the world, but was revealed in these last times for your sake.

The sacrifice of Christ was God's plan from the beginning. Before he created the world, God foreknew that he would send Christ. Peter's emphasis here perhaps falls on "for your sake." He wants to encourage these Christians and remind them that what the prophets and angels longed to see (vv. 10-12) has been brought to fruition for their sake. They should show their appreciation by their lives.

---

the last decade of the first century: "Let us fix our attention on the blood of Christ and realize that it is precious to his Father because, poured out for our salvation, it brought the grace of repentance to the whole world." 1 Clement 7.4.

[27]E.g., Davids, *First Epistle*, pp. 72-73.

[28]So Achtemeier, *1 Peter*, pp. 128-129.

1:21 Through him you believe in God, who raised him from the dead and glorified him, and so your faith and hope are in God.

Peter's overall goal is to help his audience to maintain their faith and hope. God's resurrection and glorification (= exaltation?) of Jesus are a firm basis for both. Note that the paragraph comes full circle beginning with calling upon God as Father and ending with faith and hope in God.

E. LOVE ONE ANOTHER AS THOSE BORN AGAIN THROUGH THE WORD OF GOD (1:22-25)

[22]Now that you have purified yourselves by obeying the truth so that you have sincere love for your brothers, love one another deeply, from the heart.[a] [23]For you have been born again, not of perishable seed, but of imperishable, through the living and enduring word of God. [24]For,

> **"All men are like grass,**
> **and all their glory is like the flowers of the field;**
> **the grass withers and the flowers fail,**
> **[25]but the word of the Lord stands forever."[b]**

And this is the word that was preached to you.

[a]22 Some early manuscripts *from a pure heart*   [b]25 Isaiah 40:6-8

Peter does not address these Christians as isolated individuals, but as a community of believers. This section marks the beginning of a repeated emphasis on relationships within the church. As they face persecution and distress from without, it is vital that they maintain mutual support from within. The majority of this paragraph, however, is not given to the imperative to love, but to the rationale behind it. They should love one another because they have purified their souls by obeying the truth and have been born again through the word of God.

1:22 Now that you have purified yourselves by obeying the truth so that you have sincere love for your brothers,

The words used for purification have the same root as those used for sanctification and have a similar meaning. They are usually used for ritual purification in connection with Old Testament rites. Here the word "purify" has a moral overtone. What we need to be purified from is sin. (The NIV's "yourselves" is a legitimate translation of "your souls," since Peter is not thinking of a part of the human being, but uses "soul" in a more holistic sense [cf. v. 9].) Obedience to the truth brings about this purification. Verses 23-25 indicate that by "the truth" Peter means the gospel message.[29]

The result of being purified by obedience is a sincere love of the brothers.[30] An explanation of this point may be found in 2:1. Purification involves getting rid of those things that interfere with sincere love: deceit, hypocrisy, envy, and slander. Those who purify themselves of these things can have a sincere love for each other.

love one another deeply, from the heart.

Peter's words about their obedience resulting in sincere love is not simply a description of what has happened, but a basis for appealing for a deep mutual love. They need to be who they are. They need to put their faith into practice with each other. The rest of the letter will often emphasize the importance of relationships within the community of faith. The adverb ἐκτενῶς (ektenōs) translated "deeply" might also be translated, as in the NRSV footnote, "constantly."[31]

---

[29]The majority of late manuscripts add "through the spirit" after "obeying the truth." There are other minor textual variants at this point.

[30]The word translated "love for your brothers" is φιλαδελφία (philadelphia). BAGD, p. 858, says that outside of the New Testament it was used "in the literal sense of love for blood brothers or sisters."

[31]Both the NIV and NRSV relegate to a footnote a small addition which the UBS4 editors favor mildly: from a *pure* heart.

1:23 For you have been born again, not of perishable seed, but of imperishable, through the living and enduring word of God.

On the metaphor of new birth see the comments on verse 3. The use of this metaphor here in verse 23 is closely tied to 2:1-2: you have been born again, so get rid of the evil ways of the past and, like newborn babies, crave the pure spiritual milk.

The new spiritual birth was not conceived like the first physical birth. The seed from which the new birth is conceived is not perishable (like a father's seed) but imperishable. Like the Christian's imperishable inheritance (1:4) and like the value of Christ's precious blood (contrasted in vv. 18-19 with perishable silver and gold), the word of God will stand forever.[32] That word is identified in verse 25 as the gospel that was preached to Peter's audience.

1:24 For, "All men are like grass, and all their glory is like the flowers of the field; the grass withers and the flowers fall, 1:25 but the word of the Lord stands forever."

The citation of Isaiah 40:6-8[33] helps Peter underscore the imperishable nature of God's word.[34] The primary point Peter wants to take from the quotation is that "the word of the Lord stands forever." The Christians of Asia Minor were right to be obedient to it.

And this is the word that was preached to you.

Peter identifies the word he has in mind as the gospel they had heard.

---

[32]It is grammatically possible to take "living and enduring" in verse 23 as modifying "God" rather than "the word," as in the NRSV footnote. The context of verses 24-25 suggests that they modify "the word."

[33]The citation primarily follows the Septuagint (Greek) text rather than the Masoretic (Hebrew) Text. The Septuagint and 1 Peter leave out verse 7 of the Hebrew text.

[34]Although the Greek word for "word" used in the quotation (ῥῆμα, *rhēma*) differs from the one in verse 23 (λόγος, *logos*), the context indicates that Peter has the same referent in mind.

1 PETER 2

F. CRAVE PURE SPIRITUAL MILK (2:1-3)

¹**Therefore, rid yourselves of all malice and all deceit, hypocrisy, envy, and slander of every kind. ²Like newborn babies, crave pure spiritual milk, so that by it you may grow up in your salvation, ³now that you have tasted that the Lord is good.**

This paragraph, a single sentence in the Greek text, continues the emphasis on love and the appeal to the new birth that were begun in the previous paragraph. The exhortation to "love one another deeply" is continued by an exhortation to get rid of those attitudes that destroy loving relationships. The new birth analogy is carried further with a metaphorical use of babies' cravings for milk.

2:1 Therefore, rid yourselves of all malice and all deceit, hypocrisy, envy, and slander of every kind.

The conjunction "therefore" appeals to these Christians' experience of having been born again through the living and enduring word of God (1:23). Because they have been born again through the preaching of the gospel, they need to lay aside whatever is contrary to sincere (cf. 1:22) love for one another. The word used for the first vice (κακία, *kakia*), is sometimes used broadly of wickedness or vice in general, but in this context presumably has the narrower connotation "malice, ill-will."[1] The third vice, hypocrisy (ὑπόκρισις, *hypokrisis*), is

---

[1] *BAGD* p. 397.

the opposite of the word "sincere" (ἀνυπόκριτος, *anypokritos*) in 1:22. Sincere love is diametrically opposed to malice, deceit, hypocrisy, envy, and slander. The use of the Greek word for "all" (or "every") divides the list into three groups as seen in the NRSV: "all malice, and all guile, insincerity, envy, and all slander." Although Christians should of course avoid these vices in contact with those of the world as well, the context indicates Peter is addressing this group about their relationships with each other (cf. 1:22).

2:2 Like newborn babies, crave pure spiritual milk,

Peter resumes the new birth metaphor of 1:23 (cf. 1:3) and extends it to urge his audience to center their lives on the gospel. As a newborn baby cries out for the nourishment of its mother's milk, so Christians should yearn for the nourishment of the word of God. The use of this metaphor does not presume that all the addressees are recent converts, but simply that all Christians may be compared to newborn infants in their need for spiritual milk. It is important not to confuse Peter's use of the metaphors of milk and infancy with the use of these metaphors in Hebrews 5:12-14 (cf. 1 Cor 3:1-3), where milk is contrasted with solid food and infancy is contrasted with maturity. Peter makes no reference to such contrasts. In his metaphor all Christians are like infants and all of God's word is spiritual milk. His point is that every Christian should long for the word of God like a newborn longs for milk.

Peter does not explicitly define what he symbolizes as milk. The usual understanding is that he means the word of God.[2] This is supported contextually by the references to the word of God (= the gospel) in 1:23-25. It may also be supported by the metaphorical use of milk for the word of God elsewhere, for example 1 Corinthians 3:1-3 and Hebrews 5:12-14, although I have already noted that the metaphor is used differently in

---

[2]So, e.g., Achtemeier, *1 Peter*, pp. 146-147; Davids, *First Epistle*, p. 82.

these cases in which milk only stands for certain elementary aspects of God's word. The idea that the word of God is the means by which one grows into salvation (see the next clause in 2:2) would be parallel to James 1:21: "the implanted word that has the power to save your souls" (NRSV). It is probable that milk in 1 Peter 2:2 refers to the word of God, but it is uncertain. Michaels may be correct in suggesting that "the medium by which the milk is received is the proclaimed message of the gospel, but the milk itself is more appropriately interpreted as the sustaining life of God given in mercy to his children."[3] The difference involved in his view is not great.

This milk is described as "pure" and "spiritual." In the Greek text the first adjective (ἄδολος, *adolos*, "pure" or "without deceit") clearly contrasts with the second attitude verse 1 says Christians should get rid of (δόλος, *dolos*, "deceit"). The word (λογικός, *logikos*) translated "spiritual" is problematic. Achtemeier supports the KJV rendering "milk of the word," which would of course clarify what Peter means by milk (see the previous paragraph).[4] Most recent translations and interpreters support the translation "spiritual."[5] Peter may intend the connotation "metaphorical milk" as opposed to "literal milk."[6]

so that by it you may grow up in your salvation,

Just as an infant longs for milk as nourishment to grow to adulthood, so the Christian longs for the word of God, the gospel, in order to grow "into salvation" (the more literal translation of the NRSV). Presumably by "salvation" Peter has in mind the same referent as in 1:5, "the salvation that is ready to be revealed in the last time," and 1:9, "the goal of your faith, the salvation of your souls." By drinking the pure

---

[3]Michaels, *1 Peter*, pp. 88-89.
[4]Achtemeier, *1 Peter*, pp. 146-147.
[5]So the NIV; NRSV; Davids, *First Epistle*, pp. 82-83; Michaels, *1 Peter*, pp. 87-88; and *BAGD*, p. 476.
[6]*BAGD*, p. 476.

spiritual milk of the gospel, Christians grow spiritually and maintain their hope of salvation.

2:3 now that you have tasted that the Lord is good.

The Christians of Asia Minor should long for the gospel like a baby longs for milk because they have already tasted how good the Lord is. How could anyone who has taken even a sip from the kindness of the Lord resist drinking more? The language alludes to Psalm 34:8.[7] The psalmist exhorts others to "taste and see that the LORD is good." Peter assumes these Christians have already tasted that goodness.

In this verse "the Lord" means Christ: "the Lord" is clearly the antecedent of the "living Stone — rejected by men but chosen by God" in verse 4.

G. GOD'S CHOSEN PEOPLE THROUGH JESUS (2:4-10)

[4]As you come to him, the living Stone — rejected by men but chosen by God and precious to him — [5]you also, like living stones, are being built into a spiritual house to be a holy priesthood, offering spiritual sacrifices acceptable to God through Jesus Christ. [6]For in Scripture it says:

"See, I lay a stone in Zion,
a chosen and precious cornerstone,
and the one who trusts in him
will never be put to shame."[a]

[7]Now to you who believe, this stone is precious. But to those who do not believe,

"The stone the builders rejected
has become the capstone,[b]"[c]

[8]and

---

[7]1 Peter 3:10-12 cites Psalm 34:12-16.

**"A stone that causes men to stumble
and a rock that makes them fall."**^d

They stumble because they disobey the message — which is
also what they were destined for.

**⁹But you are a chosen people, a royal priesthood, a holy
nation, a people belonging to God, that you may declare the
praises of him who called you out of darkness into his wonderful light. ¹⁰Once you were not a people, but now you are
the people of God; once you had not received mercy, but
now you have received mercy.**

ᵃ6 Isaiah 28:16   ᵇ7 Or *cornerstone*   ᶜ7 Psalm 118:22   ᵈ8 Isaiah 8:14

Each of the previous four paragraphs has focused on
exhortations built upon imperatives: "be holy in all you do,"
"live in reverent fear," "love one another," and "crave pure
spiritual milk." Immediately after the section at hand (2:4-10),
2:11-12 begins another series of exhortations.

The NRSV translators and a number of interpreters
believe that 2:4-5 should also be understood imperatively:
"Come to him, . . . let yourselves be built into a spiritual
house."[8] However, the NIV translators and other interpreters
believe 2:4-5 are a declarative statement: "As you come to
him, . . . you . . . are being built into a spiritual house."[9] The
decision is not an easy one. The key item in the discussion is
that the verb οἰκοδομεῖσθε (*oikodomeisthe*) translated "let yourselves be built" or "you are being built" has a form that may
be either imperative (the NRSV translation) or indicative (the
NIV). I am hesitantly inclined to agree with the NIV and the

---

[8]So James Moffatt, *The General Epistles*, MNTC (New York: Harper and
Brothers, 1940), p. 114; Charles Bigg, *Epistles of St. Peter and St. Jude*, ICC
(Edinburgh: T & T Clark, 1901), p. 128; and Goppelt, *Commentary*, p. 144.

[9]So most recent commentators: Michaels, *1 Peter*, p. 100; Davids, *First
Epistle*, p. 87; I Howard Marshall, *1 Peter*, IVP New Testament Commentary
Series (Downers Grove, IL: InterVarsity, 1991), p. 66; and Achtemeier,
1 Peter, p. 155.

majority of recent commentators and treat 2:4-5 as a declarative statement.

If this is correct, then 2:4-10 and 1:1-12 are the only sections of the book that are not built around imperatives or exhortations. They are foundation pieces for the exhortations found throughout the remainder of the book. It should not be overlooked that throughout the paragraphs that center on imperatives there are frequent statements about the grounds for Peter's exhortations. But the greeting (1:1-2), the opening blessing (1:3-12), and the present section (2:4-10) have a special significance in this regard. The earlier section, 1:3-12, focused on the hope of salvation that Christians may look forward to. This present passage, 2:4-10, focuses on the fact that Christians are God's chosen people. Both of these focal points are foundational for Peter's appeals. Modern Christians can also gain great motivation by focusing on our eternal hope and on our identity as God's own people.

2:4 As you come to him, the living Stone — rejected by men but chosen by God and precious to him —

Peter builds 2:4-10 around stone and building imagery. Jesus began the use of this metaphor by his appropriation of Psalm 118:22 ("The stone the builders rejected has become the capstone" — cited by Jesus in Matthew 21:42 and parallels). According to Acts 4:11 Peter used this same reference when he and John were brought to trial before the Sanhedrin. In Romans 9:32-33 Paul referred to stone imagery taken from Isaiah 8:14 and 28:16. In 2:4-10 Peter uses all three Old Testament texts and carries the imagery further.

He enhances the metaphor by describing Jesus as a "living" stone. In verse 5 he will describe his audience as "living" stones. Their participation in the spiritual house of God is through Jesus ("As you come to him").

The first clause describing Jesus, "rejected by men," reflects Psalm 118:22, which Peter will cite in verse 7. The second clause, "but chosen by God and precious to him," reflects Isaiah

28:16, which Peter will cite in verse 6. Like their Lord, the Christians in Asia Minor were also rejected by men, but chosen and precious to God. Peter described them as elect or chosen in the greeting of the letter and he will describe them again with that term in verse 9 ("a chosen people").

2:5 you also, like living stones, are being built into a spiritual house

Here Peter extends the stone metaphor to his audience. Like Jesus they are living stones. God is building them into a spiritual house.[10] Ancient readers, whether Jewish or pagan in background, would recognize this as a reference to a temple, especially in the context of priests and sacrifices (see the rest of the verse). Peter is not the only New Testament author to describe the church as a temple. It is a common idea found also in 1 Corinthians 3:16-17; 2 Corinthians 6:16; 1 Timothy 3:15; Hebrews 3:6; 10:21; and especially Ephesians 2:19-22. The adjective "spiritual" may refer both to the fact that the house Peter has in mind is not a literal one and to the fact that God's Spirit dwells in it.[11]

to be a holy priesthood, offering spiritual sacrifices acceptable to God through Jesus Christ.

Peter shifts metaphors. He first described Christians as the living stones being built into a spiritual temple. Now he immediately shifts to describe Christians as the priests who offer sacrifices in the temple.[12]

This is the classic text for the Protestant doctrine of the priesthood of all believers: that all Christians, rather than just

---

[10]On the question of whether the verb for building is an imperative or indicative see the above introductory comments to 2:4-10.

[11]Michaels, *1 Peter*, p. 100.

[12]The shift may rely partially on the fact that the Greek word for "house" (οἶκος, *oikos*) can be used both for a building and for its inhabitants. The English word "house" can also be used in the latter sense: e.g., "As for me and my house, we will serve the LORD."

select Christians, are priests. The doctrine is true, but it is not Peter's point. He is not dealing with Christians' equality with each other, but with the fact that Christians are God's chosen servants, set apart ("holy" — see 1:16) by God to offer spiritual sacrifices to him.

Just as a major purpose of the Old Testament priesthood was to offer sacrifices, so the purpose of Christians as priests is to offer sacrifices.[13] The idea of "spiritual" sacrifices has roots in the Old Testament (e.g., Ps 51:16-17; Micah 6:6-8) and appears elsewhere in the New Testament (e.g., Rom 12:1; Heb 13:15-16). Peter does not specify particular acts that he has in mind as spiritual sacrifices. Verse 9 ("you are . . . a royal priesthood . . . that you may declare the praises of him who called you") suggests one possibility.[14] The book of 1 Peter is full of possibilities. Virtually everything he exhorts his readers to do could be considered a spiritual sacrifice.

It is through Christ that Christians can offer up spiritual sacrifices that are acceptable to God. The idea of acceptable vs. unacceptable sacrifices is found in the Old and New Testament texts cited above as parallels to the notion of spiritual sacrifices.

2:6 For in Scripture it says: "See, I lay a stone in Zion, a chosen and precious cornerstone, and the one who trusts in him will never be put to shame."

Verses 6-8 provide the Scriptures behind verse 4 and Peter's use of the stone imagery for Christ. Peter reverses the order of texts alluded to in verse 4. The last clause of verse 4 stated that the living Stone was "chosen by God and precious to him": verse 6 cites the text Peter had in mind. That text is Isaiah 28:16, also cited in Romans 9:33.[15]

---

[13]The NRSV translation "to offer spiritual sacrifices" correctly conveys the infinitive of purpose.

[14]So Achtemeier, *1 Peter*, pp. 157-158.

[15]Peter and Paul cite forms of Isaiah 28:16 that do not match our available Hebrew or Greek texts nor each other. See Achtemeier, *1 Peter*, p. 159.

The NIV translates the type of stone as a "cornerstone." The Greek word ἀκρογωνιαῖος (*akrogōniaios*, "extreme corner") so translated is unknown outside of Isaiah 28:16 and Christian writings. In verse 7 the NIV's "capstone" translates a two word phrase, κεφαλὴν γωνίας (*kephalēn gōnias*, "head of the corner"), the meaning of which is also disputed. As the NIV translation of verse 7 indicates, some believe one or both of these references refer to a capstone at the top of a building or a keystone at the top of an arch. However, according to verse 8 unbelievers stumble over it. Apparently it sits on the ground, which suggests a cornerstone.[16]

The last clause in verse 6 and the first clause in verse 7 highlight the value of the living Stone for those who believe in him. Verses 7b-8 focus on the living Stone as a threat to those who do not believe.

2:7 Now to you who believe, this stone is precious.

The living Stone is precious not only to God, but also to those who believe in him. The last part of the previous verse indicates why: "the one who trusts in him will never be put to shame."

But to those who do not believe, "The stone the builders rejected has become the capstone,"

Verses 7b-8 take up the meaning of the living Stone for those who do not believe. Peter cites Psalm 118:22, a text which Jesus himself had cited (Matt 21:42 and parallels) and which Peter had cited before the Sanhedrin (Acts 4:11). In those earlier contexts the builders were the Jewish leadership in Palestine. In 1 Peter they are the non-Christians in Asia Minor. Despite their rejection of Jesus, he has become the cornerstone of God's house.[17]

---

[16]So also most recent interpreters. See Achtemeier, *1 Peter*, pp. 159-160.

[17]Concerning "cornerstone" versus the NIV's "capstone," see the comments on verse 6.

2:8 and, "A stone that causes men to stumble and a rock that makes them fall." They stumble because they disobey the message, which is also what they were destined for.

To describe the import of Jesus for those who reject him, Peter cites or alludes to[18] Isaiah 8:14. The Stone the builders rejected will cause them to fall. They will stumble and fall because they disobey the word.

The last clause raises the question of predestination. A key issue is the antecedent of the relative pronoun "which." Perhaps Peter's point is that those who disobey the message are predestined to stumble.[19] He does not necessarily mean that they were predestined to disobey. Perhaps he also means that in a corporate — not individual — sense God predestined that some would disobey.[20] In any case it seems clear that Peter holds those who disobey responsible for their actions.[21]

2:9 But you are a chosen people, a royal priesthood, a holy nation, a people belonging to God,

In contrast to those who disobey and stumble, Peter's addressees have believed and obeyed and thus become God's chosen people. Verses 9-10 provide the culmination of verses 4-10.

The four descriptions Peter uses are rooted in Exodus 19:6a and Isaiah 43:20-21.[22] The first phrase is preferably translated "chosen race" (as in the NRSV).[23] This phrase

---

[18]Achtemeier, *1 Peter*, p. 161, points out that Peter's words differ significantly from both the Hebrew and Greek (LXX) texts. They are most similar to Paul's use of Isaiah 8:14 in Romans 9:33.

[19]So Michaels, *1 Peter*, p. 107.

[20]So Davids, *First Epistle*, p. 90.

[21]Achtemeier, *1 Peter*, p. 163.

[22]Exodus 19:6a: "you will be for me a kingdom of priests and a holy nation." Isaiah 43:20c-21: ". . . my people, my chosen, the people I formed for myself that they may proclaim my praise."

[23]Here Peter uses γένος (*genos*, "race"), not λαός (*laos*, "people"). He uses *laos* later in this verse and in verse 10.

comes from Isaiah 43:20 where it describes Israel. Peter uses it to describe God's new people.

The second phrase, "a royal priesthood," is drawn from Exodus 19:6a and contains some ambiguity. The Hebrew text of Exodus 19:6a literally means "a kingdom of priests." The Septuagint translators did not translate it literally. Peter follows the Septuagint. What did he mean by the phrase in his context? A few believe that Peter intended two separate descriptions: "a king's house, a priesthood."[24] However, in view of the structure of the three accompanying phrases, it appears likely that he meant the first word as an adjective, thus "a royal priesthood." By royal priesthood he meant a group of priests in special service of the king, that is, God.

The third phrase, "a holy nation," also comes from Exodus 19:6a. Like the old people of God, the nation of Israel, the new people of God are a nation of people set apart for the service of God.

The fourth phrase, "a people belonging to God," expresses a similar idea. It is rooted in the Septuagint of Isaiah 43:21, which speaks of "my people whom I have acquired."

These four phrases take language first applied to Israel and apply it to the Christians in Asia Minor. Verse 10 will highlight the main point: once they were no people, but now they are God's people.

that you may declare the praises of him who called you out of darkness into his wonderful light.

Peter continues to follow Isaiah 43:20-21, from which he has taken the descriptions, "a chosen race" and "a people belonging to God." God says in Isaiah that he acquired Israel as his people "that they may proclaim my praise." The purpose of God's people is to declare his praises. The word ἀρετάς (aretas)

---

[24]J.H. Elliott, *The Elect and the Holy: An Exegetical Examination of 1 Peter 2:4-10 and the Phrase* βασίλειον ἱεράτευμα, Novum Testamentum Supplement 12 (Leiden: Brill, 1966).

translated "praises" should perhaps be translated, as in the NRSV, "mighty acts."[25]

2:10 Once you were not a people, but now you are the people of God; once you had not received mercy, but now you have received mercy.

This ultimate climax of 2:4-10 is rooted in Hosea 2:23: "I will show my love to the one I called 'Not my loved one.' I will say to those called 'Not my people,' 'You are my people.'" In the Septuagint text the word the NIV translates "love" is the same Greek word that in our verse is translated "received mercy." Peter does not quote Hosea, but he uses Hosea's language and concepts to describe how his readers have been called out of darkness and into light. By God's mercy they are now God's people. The wonder of this transformation should help them face the struggles they are having.

III. INSTRUCTIONS FOR EXEMPLARY LIVING IN SOCIETY'S STRUCTURES (2:11–3:12)

A. LIVE GOOD LIVES AMONG THE PAGANS (2:11-12)

[11]**Dear friends, I urge you, as aliens and strangers in the world, to abstain from sinful desires, which war against your soul.** [12]**Live such good lives among the pagans that, though they accuse you of doing wrong, they may see your good deeds and glorify God on the day he visits us.**

The NIV places a subheading after these verses, linking them more strongly to the preceding section. They do contain concepts brought up as early as 1:1 (where Peter first describes his readers as "strangers"), and they express the exhortation for which Peter has laid the foundation by

---

[25]Cf. *BAGD*, p. 106.

describing his readers as God's people who are to declare his praises (2:4-10).

However, most interpreters correctly argue that these verses function primarily as an introduction to the following paragraphs in which Peter takes up how Christians should relate to the (non-Christian) state, how Christian slaves should relate to their masters (especially non-Christian ones), and how Christian wives and husbands should relate to their spouses (especially Christian wives to non-Christian husbands). In addition to the clear contextual connection of 2:11-12 with what follows, Peter's interjection of "Dear friends" (here and in 4:12) is perhaps an indication of the beginning of a new section.

2:11 Dear friends, I urge you, as aliens and strangers in the world,

"Dear friends" translates ἀγαπητοί (*agapētoi*), literally "beloved." This is a common term in the New Testament, used first of Jesus as God's "beloved" Son and then of Christians. It presumably expresses primarily Peter's relationship to his readers (cf. 1 Thess 2:8, "you had become so dear [beloved] to us"), but may also connote the fact that they are loved by God.[26]

As Peter exhorts his readers, he describes them as "aliens and strangers in the world." See 1:1 for Peter's previous use of the word translated "strangers in the world." There he associated that concept with a metaphorical use of the Jewish Diaspora. Here he uses the accompanying term "aliens." The two words have a similar meaning, although "aliens" often referred to "resident aliens," while "strangers" often referred to temporary sojourners. The combination of the two words reflects the language of the Septuagint of Genesis 23:4 (where Abraham describes himself as an alien and a stranger among the Hittites) and Psalm 39:12 (Septuagint 38:13, in which the

---

[26]Cf. Michaels, *1 Peter*, p. 115.

psalmist describes himself as an alien and stranger). Peter's idea is a powerful one: Christians are exiles on the earth. Their true citizenship is in heaven.

to abstain from sinful desires, which war against your soul.

Christians are to purposefully maintain their status as aliens and refuse to adopt the culture of their neighbors. That culture is characterized by "the desires of the flesh." Galatians 5:16-21 provides a description of the desires of the flesh: for example, sexual immorality, impurity, idolatry, hatred, jealousy, drunkenness, orgies, etc. Peter has already indicated (1:14,18) that his readers participated in these activities in the past. He will be more specific about this in 4:3: "You have spent enough time in the past doing what pagans choose to do — living in debauchery, lust, drunkenness, orgies, carousing and detestable idolatry."

These things "war against your soul." The use of the metaphor of spiritual warfare is found in several places in the New Testament, most notably Ephesians 6:10-17. Here as elsewhere, Peter uses the word "soul" for the whole human person and not to identify a certain spiritual part of the whole (see the comments at 1:9 and 22).

2:12 Live such good lives among the pagans that, though they accuse you of doing wrong, they may see your good deeds and glorify God on the day he visits us.

The word here translated "pagan" (ἔθνος, *ethnos*) is often translated "Gentile." In many occurrences it means "non-Jew" (e.g., Acts 14:2). Because of the immoral behavior of most non-Jews, the Jews also used it to connote immorality.[27] Peter uses it here and in 4:3 in a way that differentiates between his readers, most of whom were non-Jews, and the immoral people they lived among. "Pagan" is a good translation. His readers had once been pagans, but they had ceased that lifestyle.

---

[27]*BAGD*, p. 218.

Examples of how pagans might accuse Christians of wrongdoing are provided in the following paragraphs of 1 Peter. They might be accused of undermining governing authorities (2:13-17). Christian slaves might be accused of failing to submit to their masters (2:18-25). Christian wives might be accused of being rebellious against pagan husbands (3:1-6). Beyond 1 Peter there are numerous examples of ancient pagan criticisms of Christians. In the New Testament see, for example, Acts 16:20-21; 19:23-29. See also the pagan references cited in the "Introduction to 1 Peter."[28] Those who live their lives in opposition to the prevailing culture pay a price.

The statement "they may see your good deeds and glorify God" is similar to Jesus' Sermon on the Mount: "that they may see your good deeds and praise your Father in heaven" (Matt 5:16). The section 2:13–3:7 provides examples of the good works Peter encourages.

"On the day he visits us" is a difficult phrase. In other biblical texts the day or time of God's visitation may be used either in a good sense (e.g., Luke 19:44) or to refer to a time of judgment (e.g., Isa 10:3; Jer 6:15). Michaels and others believe Peter is referring to the day of judgment.[29] As Michaels explains it, the idea is that the slandering pagans will be led to conversion and therefore when the day of judgment comes they will glorify God for the good works that led them to salvation.[30] Selwyn and others believe the day of visitation is a time during human history, a day of conversion in the lives of some pagans.[31] Both of these views coincide in seeing a missionary purpose for Christians' good works. Others, for example Achtemeier, agree with Michaels that the day is the day of judgment, but do not believe Peter is talking about pagans

---

[28]In the subsection entitled "Encouraging the Persecuted," pp. 18-19.

[29]Michaels, *1 Peter*, pp. 118-120; cf. the NRSV translation, "when he comes to judge."

[30]Ibid.

[31]Selwyn, *First Peter*, p. 171; Marshall, *1 Peter*, p. 87.

who have been converted glorifying God. Rather, in his view
Peter means that the pagans who slandered Christians while
on earth will see the truth and glorify God on the day of judgment. For the notion that even the condemned will glorify
God at judgment, he refers to Philippians 2:10-11.[32] But 1 Peter
3:1-2 seems to support a missionary view.

B. SUBMIT TO THE GOVERNING AUTHORITIES
(2:13-17)

**[13]Submit yourselves for the Lord's sake to every authority
instituted among men: whether to the king, as the supreme
authority, [14]or to governors, who are sent by him to punish
those who do wrong and to commend those who do right.
[15]For it is God's will that by doing good you should silence
the ignorant talk of foolish men. [16]Live as free men, but do
not use your freedom as a cover-up for evil; live as servants
of God. [17]Show proper respect to everyone: Love the brotherhood of believers, fear God, honor the king.**

In 2:13–3:7 Peter provides specifics of what it means to
live good lives among the pagans. He addresses three societal
structures: the individual and the government, slaves and
masters, and husbands and wives.

First Peter 2:13-17 is similar to Romans 13:1-7. Both take a
relatively positive view of governmental authorities. Peter was,
of course, not ignorant of occasions when governing authorities sought to compel Christians to violate God's will and
needed to be resisted (cf. Acts 4:19). But he does write at a
time different from that of the book of Revelation, when it
appears an emperor (Domitian?) was imposing emperor worship on the Christians in Asia Minor. Peter's views should be

---

[32]Achtemeier, *1 Peter*, p. 178, especially notes 82-83.

understood as general truths: on the whole governing authorities are a good thing, and Christians should submit to them.
He does not deal with the exceptions. (The same could be
said of Paul in Romans 13.)

2:13 Submit yourselves for the Lord's sake to every authori-
ty instituted among men:

Peter's exhortation to Christians in relationship to government, slaves in relationship to masters, and wives in relationship to husbands is the same: submit. This, of course, does not
mean that Peter did not have differing conceptions of the
nature of the submission involved in each case. Just as Peter
would certainly see a difference between the nature of the
honor involved in 2:17 when he says "honor everyone" and
"honor the king,"[33] he would also see a difference between the
submission that citizens owe to their rulers and the submission
that slaves owe to masters. Nevertheless, all three relationships
that he describes involve authority and submission.[34]

The three Greek words translated "every authority instituted among men" (πάσῃ ἀνθρωπίνῃ κτίσει, *pasē anthrōpinē kti-
sei*) are not clear. The NIV translation reflects the common
view that the context calls for a reference to institutions of
government, but it is hard to demonstrate that these Greek

---

[33]The NIV translation obscures the fact that the same verb is used in the
first and last clauses of 2:17.

[34]Several interpreters provide discussions of the differences in meaning
they see for various English translations of the verb ὑποτάσσω (*hypotasso*);
such as "submit," "be subordinate," "accept the authority of," or "show def-
erence to." In my opinion these English words have varying connotations
from one person to another and one context to another. Peter uses one
Greek verb to cover differing kinds of "submission" (or whatever one
chooses to call it). Paul, on the other hand, seems to make distinctions in
Colossians 3:18-25 and Ephesians 5:22–6:9 by using Peter's verb for wives
and a stronger verb (ὑπακούω, *hypakouo*, obey) for the role of children and
slaves. Even Paul does not make consistent use of these distinctions. In
1 Timothy 2:5,9 he uses Peter's verb for both wives and slaves. The English
verb "submit," like Peter's Greek verb, has a wide range of meanings and
may be used as a suitable English equivalent for Peter's verb.

words can mean that.[35] The primary alternative, one clearly supported for these words, is "every human creature" — but that is more difficult to fit into the context. It is possible, however, that Peter means "submit to every human creature" and then identifies the particular persons he has in mind as rulers.[36] There is a parallel to this flow of thought in 2:17: "Honor everyone. . . . Honor the emperor" (NRSV translation). If Peter means "human creature," he may have chosen this odd-seeming phrase in deliberate contrast to those who would view the emperor as more than human. However this difficult phrase is translated, the focus of the paragraph is on the submission due to rulers.

Christians are to submit to rulers "for the Lord's sake." Verse 15 expands on why the Lord is interested in such behavior: "it is God's will that by doing good you should silence the ignorant talk of foolish men."

whether to the king as the supreme authority,

The earlier phrase "for the Lord's sake" implies who Peter believes the ultimate supreme authority is. It also implicitly qualifies the obedience due to the earthly supreme authority. The king Peter has in mind is the emperor of Rome.

2:14 or to governors, who are sent by him to punish those who do wrong and to commend those who do right.

Between the provinces of Asia Minor and the emperor himself were the governors of the provinces, who were sent by the emperor to oversee the day-to-day matters of government. Even secular sources would agree that one of their chief purposes was to punish those who do wrong and commend those who do right.[37] As noted above in the comments

---

[35]See *BAGD*, pp. 455-456 under "κτίσις," for an attempt.

[36]So Michaels, *1 Peter*, p. 124; Davids, *First Epistle*, pp. 98-99; Achtemeier, *1 Peter*, pp. 182-183.

[37]See the references in Achtemeier, *1 Peter*, p. 184, n. 55.

introducing this section, Peter was not naively ignorant of exceptions to this goal. He speaks in generalities.

The letter of 1 Peter has a strong emphasis on doing right vs. doing wrong: see 2:15,20; 3:6,10-12,13-14,17; 4:18-19.

2:15 For it is God's will that by doing good you should silence the ignorant talk of foolish men.

Peter introduced this section by exhorting his readers to live lives that will prove their accusers wrong. His hope, of course, is not only that their opponents will "be put to shame" (3:16), but also that some among them might "be won over" (3:1).

2:16 Live as free men, but do not use your freedom as a cover-up for evil; live as servants of God.

In the Greek text 2:13-16 is all a single sentence and the main verb is "submit." It would be better in breaking the sentence to resume the main verb ("submit") rather than interject one that is not there ("live"). Achtemeier provides a useful translation: "(be subordinate) as free men and women, and not as those who use their freedom as a cover for evil deeds, but as God's slaves." The notion of Christian freedom is restricted both by submission to governing authorities and by slavery to God. Several texts in the New Testament highlight the fact that Christians are "called to be free" (Gal 5:13; cf. John 8:32; Rom 6:17-18; 1 Cor 7:22; 9:19). But like 1 Peter, these same texts often go on to emphasize restrictions on that freedom and the fact that although we are free from sin, law, etc., we are slaves to God (e.g., Gal 5:13; Rom 6:18; 1 Cor 7:22). The Christians of Asia Minor have been set free from human rulers by acceptance of another Ruler. But that Ruler wants them to submit to human rulers insofar as they do not demand disobedience to his will. They must not use their Christian freedom as a "cover-up," literally a "veil" (ἐπικάλυμ–μα, *epikalymma*), for doing evil.

2:17 Show proper respect to everyone: Love the brother-hood of believers, fear God, honor the king.

As the NRSV indicates, the first and last verb are the same: "Honor everyone. . . . Honor the emperor." Their one difference is in tense, with respect to which the first verb in verse 17 differs from the other three.[38] The NIV translation suggests that one way this tense difference might be reflected is to see the first clause as an umbrella clause introducing the other three.

In the New Testament only Peter uses the term "brotherhood," although it is commonplace to find Christians identified as "brothers." Both terms are used generically to include men and women (a usage common to many languages until recently).

See the commentary on 1:17 concerning Peter's instructions to "fear God."

C. SLAVES, SUBMIT TO YOUR MASTERS (2:18-25)

1. Submit Even to Harsh Masters (2:18-20)

[18]**Slaves, submit yourselves to your masters with all respect, not only to those who are good and considerate, but also to those who are harsh. [19]For it is commendable if a man bears up under the pain of unjust suffering because he is conscious of God. [20]But how is it to your credit if you receive a beating for doing wrong and endure it? But if you suffer for doing good and you endure it, this is commendable before God.**

In Paul's letters there are two sections, Ephesians 5:22–6:9 and Colossians 3:18–4:1 (cf. Titus 2:1-10), in which he gives

---

[38]The first verb is an aorist imperative; the other three are present imperatives.

instructions to three pairs of relationships: wives and husbands, children and fathers, and slaves and masters. These relationships were the building blocks of ancient households and thus Paul's instructions concerning them are commonly labeled "household codes." There is an extensive literature on this subject and on possible precedents for the structure and content of these "codes."[39] First Peter 2:18–3:7 is similar to Paul's "household codes," although Peter does not use the same order and does not address masters or the father-child relationship. Peter is primarily concerned with his theme of "living good lives among the pagans" (2:12). Therefore he primarily addresses slaves who need encouragement to submit even to harsh masters and wives who need encouragement to submit to unbelieving husbands. (There is but one concluding sentence for husbands.) Paul's household codes are more comprehensive and also address relationships between household members in cases where they are all Christians.

2:18 Slaves, submit yourselves to your masters with all respect,

Peter addresses slaves as exemplifying those who had to make great sacrifices to "live such good lives among the pagans that, though they accuse you of doing wrong, they may see your good deeds and glorify God" (2:12). Peter's word for slave (οἰκέτης, oiketēs, "household slave") is not the usual New Testament term. It may refer specifically to slaves who worked in the house as opposed to those who worked outside the house, but it was also used for slaves in general and there is little reason to presume Peter wants to identify a certain kind of slave.

On the word "submit" see the comments on verse 13. There is a grammatical problem concerning the use of this verb here in verse 18 and again in 3:1. The NIV translation

---

[39]See Achtemeier, *1 Peter*, pp. 52-55.

("submit yourselves") accepts the common view that in these two cases a participle functions as an imperative.[40]

The NIV translation "with all respect" suggests that this prepositional phrase applies to masters. Most recent commentators argue, I think rightly, that it applies to God and should be translated something like "with all reverent fear."[41] The phrase is identical to the phrase the NIV translates "in reverent fear" in 1:17, with the addition of the word "all." Peter has just commanded his readers to "fear God" (2:17) and in the next verse (2:19) he will commend suffering because one is "conscious of God." On the fear of God as a motivation in 1 Peter see the comments on 1:17. Peter is not encouraging slaves to submit to their masters out of fear of their masters but out of the fear of God.

not only to those who are good and considerate, but also to those who are harsh.

No doubt this was extraordinarily difficult advice. Peter needed strong arguments and support if he expected slaves to willingly suffer even when they had done no wrong. This is perhaps the most difficult advice in 1 Peter and in verses 21-25 he brings up the ultimate support — the example of Christ.

2:19 For it is commendable if a man bears up under the pain of unjust suffering because he is conscious of God. 2:20 But how is it to your credit if you receive a beating for doing wrong and endure it? But if you suffer for doing good and you endure it, this is commendable before God.

A Christian slave's commitment to submitting to his or her master is truly tested when the master treats him or her harshly and unfairly. Notice the extent of the harsh treatment: not just harsh words, but a beating. This is the only specific reference to physical persecution in 1 Peter.

---

[40]See the references at chapter 1, footnote 22.

[41]So Goppelt, *Commentary*, p. 193; Michaels, *1 Peter*, p. 138; Davids, *First Epistle*, p. 106; Achtemeier, *1 Peter*, pp. 194-195.

The phrase translated "because he is conscious of God" is difficult. Some argue it means something like "because of his conscience before God."[42] The NIV reflects the more common view that the key word means something like "consciousness" rather than "conscience."[43] In either case this phrase indicates that the person patiently endures the beating because of commitment to God and not simply because he or she has no recourse. It may also suggest that the reason for the beating is something he has done out of duty to God.[44] The NIV translation of the last sentence of verse 20 is probably correct in indicating that Peter has in mind not only suffering while doing good, but suffering "for" doing good. Presumably the slave has chosen to do what is right before God against what the master has commanded or would allow.

Achtemeier rightly points out that although this section is directed to slaves, "they and their fate stand as exemplary both of the Christian's situation in the Roman Empire and of the Christlike reaction they must adopt to it."[45] All Christians should learn from Peter's advice to slaves.

2. Follow the Example of Christ (2:21-25)

[21]**To this you were called, because Christ suffered for you, leaving you an example, that you should follow in his steps.**

[22]**"He committed no sin,**
and no deceit was found in his mouth."[a]

[23]**When they hurled their insults at him, he did not retaliate; when he suffered, he made no threats. Instead, he entrusted himself to him who judges justly. [24]He himself bore our sins**

---

[42]So Davids, *First Epistle*, p. 107; Goppelt, *Commentary*, pp. 196-198.

[43]So Achtemeier, *1 Peter*, pp. 196-197; Michaels, *1 Peter*, p. 140.

[44]"The point is that the actions which cause the suffering are motivated by an awareness of what God's will is in the situation . . ." Achtemeier, *1 Peter*, p. 196. Cf. Michaels, *1 Peter*, p. 140.

[45]Achtemeier, *1 Peter*, p. 192.

in his body on the tree, so that we might die to sins and live for righteousness; by his wounds you have been healed. [25]For you were like sheep going astray, but now you have returned to the Shepherd and Overseer of your souls.

[a]*22 Isaiah 53:9*

This is actually not a new paragraph, but the completion of the paragraph encouraging slaves to submit to their masters and to endure patiently unjust suffering. Nevertheless, it has a critical importance not just to the slaves Peter directly addresses, but to all of Peter's readers and to every Christian of all generations. Therefore, it seems appropriate to single out these verses as if they constituted a separate paragraph.

As noted above, Peter needs strong support to encourage slaves to endure patiently even unjust beatings and to remain submissive. He therefore turns to the example of Christ and in the process provides one of the most compelling paragraphs of the New Testament.

2:21 To this you were called

Peter is still speaking to slaves, but every Christian reader recognizes that "you" includes all of us, just as (see the next clause) Christ suffered for us all. Peter opened the letter with a reference to the Christian's calling (the Greek word there translated "elect" is a cognate of the verb here translated "you were called"). In 1:15 he identified the One who did the calling as God and the goal of the calling as holiness. Here in verse 21 the antecedent of the word "this" is patient endurance of unjust suffering. This is an important aspect of fulfilling the call to be holy. It is an important part of the effort to "live such good lives among the pagans that . . . they may see your good deeds and glorify God . . ." (v. 12).

because Christ suffered for you,

The NIV translation omits the word "also" (NRSV: "because Christ also suffered for you"). Probably Peter used "also" because he has just used the same verb "suffer" with respect to what the slaves must endure (v. 20b).

This clause has been interpreted in two ways. Some believe that the prepositional phrase "for you" reflects the common New Testament statement that "Christ died for us" and is therefore a reference to the atoning value of Christ's suffering and death — so that your sins may be forgiven.[46] They see verse 21 as anticipating verse 24: "he himself bore our sins in his body on the tree."

Others, probably correctly, note that in verse 21 Peter does not say "Christ also *died* for you" but "Christ also *suffered* for you." They suggest that Peter is not using "for you" in the sense of "for your sins," but rather that "for you" is explained by the next part of the verse. "Christ suffered for you" means Christ suffered in order to provide you with an example to follow.[47]

leaving you an example, that you should follow in his steps.

The word ὑπογραμμόν (*hypogrammon*) translated "example" was used literally of a pattern of letters of the Greek alphabet for children to copy and thus learn to write. It was also used figuratively, as here, for a pattern for behavior.[48] Christ's suffering is a pattern for Christian slaves to follow. Jesus himself had summoned his disciples to follow him in contexts in which he discussed his coming suffering (e.g., Mark 8:31,34). Peter's wonderful addition of the phrase "in his steps" was the inspiration for the title of Charles Sheldon's famous book *In His Steps*. Christians are called to imitate Christ's willingness to suffer for doing good. He did it for us. We do it for him.

2:22 "He committed no sin, and no deceit was found in his mouth."

This citation of Isaiah 53:9 highlights the fact that Christ is

---

[46]Davids, *First Epistle*, p. 109; Goppelt, *Commentary*, p. 202.
[47]Michaels, *1 Peter*, p. 143.
[48]*BAGD*, p. 843; Michaels, *1 Peter*, p. 144; Achtemeier, *1 Peter*, p. 199.

a pattern for the type of suffering Peter endorses for Christian slaves. He did not "receive a beating for doing wrong," but rather he was one of those who "suffer for doing good" (see v. 20). Peter calls upon slaves to endure unjust suffering as innocent victims by pointing to Christ as the ultimate example of innocence.

Isaiah 53 was an important Old Testament passage in early Christian understanding of the suffering and the death of Christ (cf. the citations in Luke 22:37 and Acts 8:32-33).[49]

2:23 When they hurled their insults at him, he did not retaliate; when he suffered, he made no threats.

The pattern of Christ shows how one should endure unjust suffering for doing good. Having urged Christian slaves to submit willingly even to harsh masters and to endure patiently unjust suffering, Peter uses Jesus' behavior at his arrest, trials, and crucifixion as the example they are called to follow. He did not return insult for insult, nor did he threaten his enemies. It was surely difficult for Christian slaves to follow this example — more difficult than for the rest of us, to whom it also applies.

Peter does not use specific language reflecting Isaiah 53 in this verse. However, the clear citation of Isaiah 53 in verse 22 and the allusions in verse 24 suggest the possibility that he here alludes to Isaiah 53:7 ("He was oppressed and afflicted, yet he did not open his mouth; he was led like a lamb to the slaughter, and as a sheep before her shearers is silent, so he did not open his mouth.").

Instead, he entrusted himself to him who judges justly.

This last clause of verse 23 expands on the pattern provided by Christ's suffering. His nonretaliation reflected his trust in God. The Greek text does not specify what Jesus entrusted or delivered over to God. Some suggest he delivered over "his

---

[49]*UBS⁴* lists 32 New Testament allusions to Isaiah 53 (p. 897).

enemies";[50] others, "his cause."[51] The NIV and NRSV suggest "himself." It is a difficult decision, but the last suggestion is perhaps best in the light of 1 Peter 4:19 where Peter encourages his readers to "commit *themselves* to their faithful creator."

2:24 He himself bore our sins in his body on the tree,

If Peter was not including the death of Jesus and its atoning significance in verse 21 ("Christ suffered for you"), he clearly does now. He refers to Christ's dying for sins in order to continue to encourage his readers to "live for righteousness."

Peter's comment that "He himself bore our sins" reflects Isaiah 53:4 ("this one bears our sins"), 11 ("their sins he himself will bear"), and 12 ("he himself bore the sins of many").[52] Moving beyond Isaiah he adds that he bore those sins "in his body on the tree," clearly referring to the crucifixion. The word ξύλον (*xylon*), translated "tree," refers to wood or anything made of it. In the New Testament it is used several times for the cross (Acts 5:30; 10:39; 13:29; Gal 3:13).

so that we might die to sins and live for righteousness;

In saying we have "parted with" sins, Peter does not use the usual verb for "die to," although "die to sins" is a legitimate translation and captures the basic idea of ἀπογίνομαι (*apoginomai*).[53] The thought of the clause is similar to Romans 6:11: "count yourselves dead to sin but alive to God." Peter uses the atoning significance of Jesus' death to urge us on to do what is right.

by his wounds you have been healed.

This clause is similar in meaning to the first part of verse 24, and is likewise rooted in Isaiah 53. The last clause of

---

[50]Michaels, *1 Peter*, p. 147.

[51]J.N.D. Kelly, *A Commentary on the Epistles of Peter and of Jude*, Harper New Testament Commentary (New York: Harper and Row, 1969), p. 121.

[52]I have used Achtemeier's literal renderings of the Septuagint in order to make the allusions clearer. See Achtemeier, *1 Peter*, p. 201, n. 171.

[53]*BAGD*, p. 89. The NRSV has "so that, free from sins, . . ."

Isaiah 53:5 is "and by his wounds we are healed." Peter again points to the vicarious nature of what Jesus accomplished when he suffered and died for us. He was wounded so that we could be healed. We should therefore live righteously, which includes enduring unjust suffering for doing right.

2:25 For you were like sheep going astray, but now you have returned to the Shepherd and Overseer of your souls.

Peter reminds his readers of their past (cf. 1 Pet 1:14,18; 2:10; 4:3) in order to encourage them to stay on their new path. Sheep herding was common in the Mediterranean world and sheep/shepherd imagery is common in Scripture. In this case Peter is still following Isaiah 53. Having referred to Isaiah 53:5, he now moves on to verse 6: "We all, like sheep, have gone astray."

Peter's readers were once like lost sheep, but now they are under the care and guidance of the great Shepherd. It is doubtful that the verb "returned" implies that Peter's readers had at an earlier time been part of the great Shepherd's flock. Other statements in the book (see the verses cited in the previous paragraph) indicate that their past was in paganism.

Although in the Old Testament God is often described as the shepherd of Israel, in 1 Peter 5:4 Peter uses "chief Shepherd" with reference to Christ. He probably means Christ in this instance as well. Christ is further described as our Overseer, using the word ἐπίσκοπος (*episkopos*) often rendered in other translations as "bishop" when it refers to human overseers of the church. Peter wants his readers to follow the example of their Shepherd and Overseer.

On the word "souls" see the comments on 1:9. Peter probably does not intend a part of the person separable from the body, but rather a more holistic reference to the person. Achtemeier legitimately translates "shepherd and guardian of your lives."[54]

---

[54]Achtemeier, *1 Peter*, p. 190.

1 PETER 3

D. WIVES, SUBMIT TO YOUR HUSBANDS (3:1-6)

¹Wives, in the same way be submissive to your husbands so that, if any of them do not believe the word, they may be won over without words by the behavior of their wives, ²when they see the purity and reverence of your lives. ³Your beauty should not come from outward adornment, such as braided hair and the wearing of gold jewelry and fine clothes. ⁴Instead, it should be that of your inner self, the unfading beauty of a gentle and quiet spirit, which is of great worth in God's sight. ⁵For this is the way the holy women of the past who put their hope in God used to make themselves beautiful. They were submissive to their own husbands, ⁶like Sarah, who obeyed Abraham and called him her master. You are her daughters if you do what is right and do not give way to fear.

The changes in modern society have given new prominence to every text of Scripture that touches on relationships between men and women.[1] A growing percentage of our society has adopted the egalitarian view that in every aspect of life, including the church and home, there should be no differences in the

---

[1] Two collections of essays stand out with respect to this subject: John Piper and Wayne Grudem, eds., *Recovering Biblical Manhood and Womanhood: A Response to Evangelical Feminism* (Wheaton, IL: Crossway, 1991); and Carroll D. Osburn, ed., *Essays on Women in Earliest Christianity*, 2 vols. (Joplin, MO: College Press, 1993, 1995).

roles of men and women except those that are mandated by biology (e.g., men cannot bear children). With respect to marriage, egalitarians want to eliminate every trace of the notion that husbands should have a role of authority or leadership in the home.

Peter's comments in 1 Peter 3:1-6 create an obvious problem for this point of view. Although verse 7 indicates that Peter would not agree with the way many husbands misuse their role, he does clearly encourage Christian wives to be submissive to the leadership role of the husband.

Egalitarians usually adopt one of two views regarding Peter's comments. Some simply disagree with the author of 1 Peter (most of them would argue the author was not the apostle Peter). But those who believe Peter wrote this book and have a high view of inspiration recognize that it is not acceptable simply to disagree with Peter. They argue that Peter's advice to wives was appropriate for his culture and times, but does not necessarily apply to us. They argue that in this respect Peter's instructing wives to submit to husbands is analogous to his instructing slaves to submit to masters.

The most important objection to this "evangelical egalitarian" view is based on the writings of Paul. Paul's comments about the relationships of men and women in the church and home differ in a crucial respect from his comments about masters and slaves. In 1 Corinthians 11 and 1 Timothy 2 Paul grounds his notion of male headship in the Genesis 2 account of the creation of Adam and Eve. Paul believed that when Genesis says that God created woman for the sake of man (1 Cor 11:8-9) it implies that "the head of the woman is man" (1 Cor 11:3).[2] Peter does not comment on this "creation ordinance" view, but those of us who think Paul held it do not believe Peter would disagree.

---

[2]Concerning Paul's use of Genesis with respect to the roles of men and women, see Allan McNicol, "The Role of Women in the New Testament Doctrine of Ministry," in *Women in Earliest Christianity*, ed. Carroll D. Osburn, 2:533-539.

The view that the headship role of the husband in the home is a transcultural norm of God's will does not imply that there cannot be cultural and individual differences in how this norm is put into practice. For example, in America the wearing of veils no longer has the same symbolic meanings that it had for Paul in 1 Corinthians 11. Peter's comment that Sarah showed her submission to Abraham by calling him "lord" does not imply that every woman in Peter's day or even in Sarah's day would necessarily demonstrate their submission in the same fashion. There can be differences from one culture to another and from one marriage to another in how such a norm is carried out with respect to a myriad of details.

Peter's comments to wives are his third example of Christian submission (after submission to government and slaves' submission to masters). They constitute a second aspect of the common household structure (slaves and masters, wives and husbands, children and parents).

3:1 Wives, in the same way be submissive to your husbands

"In the same way" probably refers back to 2:13 and 18. As all Christians should submit to the governing authorities (2:13) and slaves should submit to their masters (2:18), "in the same way" wives should submit to their husbands.[3] Michaels suggests that "in the same way" is perhaps too strong, since it suggests that Peter sees no differences in the manner in which citizens, slaves, and wives submit in their various spheres.[4] He suggests "'likewise' in the sense of 'also' or 'too.'"[5]

As in 2:18, the NIV's "be submissive" follows the common view that the participle used here ("being submissive") should be translated as an imperative.[6]

---

[3]Goppelt, *Commentary*, p. 218.

[4]Michaels, *1 Peter*, pp. 156-157. See the discussion of submission in my comments on 2:13.

[5]Ibid.

[6]See the references at chapter 1, footnote 22.

Peter does not encourage wives in general to be submissive to husbands in general. He encourages each wife to submit to her own husband.

so that, if any of them do not believe the word, they may be won over without words by the behavior of their wives,

Peter's focus from the beginning of this section has been on making an impact on non-Christians: "Live such good lives among the pagans that . . . they may see your good deeds and glorify God" (2:12). Wives married to non-Christian husbands exemplify this concern.

Any wife who denied her husband's gods was apparently already violating social norms. Plutarch (a pagan writer who lived c. A.D. 50 to 120) is well known for his comment that "it is becoming for a wife to worship and know only the gods that her husband believes in, and to shut the front door tight upon all queer rituals and outlandish superstitions."[7]

Of course for Peter a wife's submission does not involve denial of Jesus Christ. But by demonstrating their submission in other areas wives may hope even to convert their non-Christian husbands.

The first use of "word" here clearly refers to the Christian gospel. The second use of "word" may involve a word play on the first. It is not used in the plural as the NIV suggests and may have a sort of double sense: "without verbal reference (a word) to the gospel (the word)."[8]

3:2 when they see the purity and reverence of your lives.

The husbands who will not listen to the gospel may yet be won over by the behavior of their wives. That behavior should be characterized by purity and reverence. The phrase translated "reverence" is literally "in fear." It is the same as the phrase translated "in reverent fear" in 1:17. Peter is not

---

[7]Plutarch *Advice to a Bride and Groom* 140D.
[8]Achtemeier, *1 Peter*, p. 210.

speaking of fear of the husband (cf. 1 Pet 3:6), but of fear of God. On the importance of this concept in 1 Peter see the comments on 1:17. Peter's observation that a Christian woman's behavior may sometimes win her husband to Christ has been proven true repeatedly throughout the centuries.

3:3 Your beauty should not come from outward adornment, such as braided hair and the wearing of gold jewelry and fine clothes.

Peter's criticism of emphasizing outward adornment is similar to Isaiah 3:16-24[9] and especially 1 Timothy 2:9-10.[10] Similar views may also be found in a variety of Greco-Roman authors who argue "that the proper attire for the woman is modesty rather than expensive garments, fancy coiffures, and jewelry."[11]

It is often and correctly stated that many contemporary Christian women (and men) do not listen to Peter or Paul on this point. Of course we should. But it is important not to misunderstand them. It is doubtful that Isaiah, Peter, or Paul meant strictly to forbid every adornment they mention. In fact in Peter's case the last item on his list is literally "clothes," not "fine clothes."[12] Just as the context implies he means "fine" clothes, so it should be understood that he means "ostentatious" braiding and gold.[13]

---

[9]"The LORD says, 'The women of Zion are haughty, walking along with outstretched necks, . . . with ornaments jingling on their ankles. . . .' In that day the LORD will snatch away their finery: the bangles and headbands and crescent necklaces, the earrings and bracelets and veils, the headdresses and . . . the linen garments and tiaras and shawls."

[10]"I also want women to dress modestly, with decency and propriety, not with braided hair or gold or pearls or expensive clothes, but with good deeds, appropriate for women who profess to worship God."

[11]This summary of the view is from Achtemeier who cites more than ten Greco-Roman authors (p. 212).

[12]Unlike 1 Timothy 2:9 in which Paul adds the modifier "expensive."

[13]Consider the matter of braiding hair. Peter presumably does not object to any and all braiding. Greco-Roman statues, paintings, etc., demonstrate

3:4 Instead, it should be that of your inner self, the unfading beauty of a gentle and quiet spirit, which is of great worth in God's sight.

The adornment of the Christian wife should be the inner self, literally "the secret person of the heart." That is where true and lasting beauty can be seen. The beauty Christian wives should have is the beauty of a gentle (or meek) and quiet spirit. In this context this spirit is a part of the concept of submission, as is seen by the explanation in verse 5 that the holy women of the past made themselves beautiful by being submissive to their husbands. Despite its lack of popularity in modern society, Peter says such a submissive, gentle, quiet spirit is very precious to God.

3:5 For this is the way the holy women of the past who put their hope in God used to make themselves beautiful. They were submissive to their own husbands,

The NRSV is preferable in showing the relationship between the parts of this verse: "the holy women who hoped in God used to adorn themselves *by* accepting the authority of their husbands." Throughout these verses Peter's emphasis is on the idea of submission. He encourages the Christian wives of Asia Minor to consider the example of faithful women from the Old Testament past. Verse 6 uses the specific example of Sarah, wife of Abraham.

3:6 like Sarah, who obeyed Abraham and called him her master.

Sarah, matriarch of the Jews, was held in high regard (cf. Heb 11:11). Peter uses her obedience to Abraham, exemplified by the way she addressed him, as an illustration of how the holy women of the past adorned themselves by submitting to their husbands. He has reference to Genesis 18:12: "So

---

that hair-braiding frequently involved elaborate styling, often incorporating expensive jewelry.

Sarah laughed to herself as she thought, 'After I am worn out and my master is old, will I now have this pleasure?'" There is little evidence to suggest that addressing a husband as "lord" or "master" was common in the time of Sarah or Peter.[14] Peter is not prescribing a particular practice, but simply providing an illustration of Sarah's submissiveness.

You are her daughters if you do what is right and do not give way to fear.

The daughters of Sarah are those who follow her example in submitting to their husbands as she did to Abraham. They remain her daughters as long as they continue to "do what is right," a concept often repeated by Peter (cf. 2:15,20; 3:10-12,13-14,17; 4:18-19). Those who do what is right have to refuse to listen to their fears of other people (cf. 3:14), including non-Christian husbands' attempts to intimidate them.

E. HUSBANDS, BE CONSIDERATE (3:7)

[7]Husbands, in the same way be considerate as you live with your wives, and treat them with respect as the weaker partner and as heirs with you of the gracious gift of life, so that nothing will hinder your prayers.

Peter's emphasis in the section beginning with 2:11 is on the submissive half of the three relationships: everyone as submissive to governing authorities, slaves as submissive to masters, and wives as submissive to husbands. With respect to household relationships, he gives no advice to masters (that there were Christian masters is clear from the writings of Paul) and only brief advice to husbands.

---

[14]Michaels, *1 Peter*, p. 164. One other example is in the Septuagint 1 Kingdoms 1:8 where Hannah addresses her husband Elkanah as "master."

3:7 Husbands, in the same way be considerate as you live with your wives,

As in 1:13, 2:18, and 3:1 the imperative verb (in this case "be considerate") is actually a participle, but may be translated as an imperative.[15]

The NIV "be considerate as you live with [your wives]" translates a prepositional phrase and a verb that could be literally translated "live with [your wives] according to knowledge." "According to knowledge" may simply mean "considerately," but in the context of 1 Peter it might have a fuller connotation, such as "according to a knowledge of what God requires."[16]

and treat them with respect as the weaker partner

Christian husbands should not take wrongful advantage of their wives being "the weaker partner," but rather should show them honor.

"Weaker partner" translates a difficult phrase. "Partner" translates the word σκεῦος (*skeuos*) used literally to mean "thing, object used for any purpose at all" or more particularly "vessel, jar, dish, etc."[17] In the New Testament it is used figuratively for Paul as a chosen instrument of God (Acts 9:15) and for the human body (2 Cor 4:7; 1 Thess 4:4). A literal translation would be "weaker vessel" (NRSV footnote; see also most older versions). Less literal translations striving to express the metaphorical meaning include the NIV's "weaker partner," the NRSV's "weaker sex," and Michaels's "somebody weaker."

More significant is the meaning of "weaker." What did Peter mean by this description? Various authors from roughly his time period can be cited to show that many believed women were weaker than men not only physically, but also

---

[15]See chapter 1, footnote 22.
[16]Achtemeier, *1 Peter*, p. 218.
[17]*BAGD*, p. 754.

intellectually and morally.[18] But in connection with his discussion of how Christian wives can convert their non-Christian husbands, Peter is unlikely to have intended to call wives weaker intellectually or morally.[19] Most recent interpreters believe he had in mind the fact that women are generally physically weaker than men and perhaps the concomitant fact that they are therefore more vulnerable to mistreatment.[20]

and as heirs with you of the gracious gift of life,

Christian husbands are to live considerately with and show honor to their wives not only in light of their weakness, but in light of the fact that they share equally in the grace of God. Peter believed in the now often denied notion that husbands and wives were equal with respect to their relationship with God, but at the same time had different and complementary roles in the home. He would agree with Paul both that "the husband is the head of the wife as Christ is the head of the church" (Eph 5:22; cf. 1 Pet 3:1-6) and that "there is no longer male and female; for all of you are one in Christ Jesus" (Gal 3:28, NRSV; cf. 1 Pet 3:7). Although spiritual equality does not negate all social differences, it does have social implications. Husbands who recognize their wives as equal partners in the grace of God must not misuse their headship of the home, but must be considerate of their wives and show them honor.

so that nothing will hinder your prayers.

There is quite a difference of opinion as to whether "your" refers only to hindering the prayers of the men directly addressed in verse 7 or also to their wives. I am inclined to agree with Achtemeier once again. He argues effectively that "The notion that God would ignore the prayers of women who are not treated in a Christian way would be to punish

---

[18]Achtemeier, *1 Peter*, p. 206.
[19]Achtemeier, *1 Peter*, p. 217; Goppelt, *Commentary*, p. 227.
[20]So, e.g., Davids, *First Epistle*, pp. 122-123.

the weak who are abused, an idea hardly in accord with
Christian tradition about the relation of God to the down-
trodden."[21] The idea that one's relationship to God may be
hindered by one's relationship to others is a repeated theme
of Scripture (cf. Matt 5:23-24; 6:12,14; Mark 11:25). Compare
also 1 Peter 4:7: "be clear minded and self-controlled so that
you can pray."

F. GENERAL INSTRUCTIONS FOR ALL (3:8-12)

[8]**Finally, all of you, live in harmony with one another; be
sympathetic, love as brothers, be compassionate and humble. [9]Do not repay evil with evil or insult with insult, but
with blessing, because to this you were called so that you
may inherit a blessing. [10]For,**

> **"Whoever would love life**
> **and see good days**
> **must keep his tongue from evil**
> **and his lips from deceitful speech.**
> [11]**He must turn from evil and do good;**
> **he must seek peace and pursue it.**
> [12]**For the eyes of the Lord are on the righteous**
> **and his ears are attentive to their prayer.**
> **But the face of the Lord is against those who do evil."[a]**

[a]*12* **Psalm 34:12-16**

This is the concluding (note the word "finally") subsection
of the major section that began with 2:11-12. Having addressed
slaves, wives, and husbands, Peter now addresses "all."

---

[21]Achtemeier, *1 Peter*, p. 218.

3:8 Finally, all of you, live in harmony with one another; be sympathetic, love as brothers, be compassionate and humble.[22]

Peter has already encouraged the Christians of Asia Minor to love each other and get rid of malice, envy, and other attitudes that might undermine their relationships (1:22–2:1). In a situation in which they face a constant struggle with outsiders, it is especially important for them to band together in love and compassion for each other.

The qualities encouraged in this verse are common features of New Testament teaching. Furthermore, although Peter does not repeat his theme verb for this section, "be submissive" (2:13,18; 3:1,5), these qualities all involve a submissive attitude.

3:9 Do not repay evil with evil or insult with insult, but with blessing,

The qualities urged in verse 8 seem to focus primarily on Christians' relationships with each other. Verse 9 can apply to how a Christian deals with other Christians, but Peter probably means to include how one deals with outsiders. Certainly that is the case in the teachings of Jesus that this advice echoes (Matt 5:38-42; Luke 6:27-28). Peter here also echoes language he has just used to describe Jesus' behavior: "When they hurled their insults at him, he did not retaliate" (2:23). This is difficult advice in the circumstances Peter addresses. He has already pointed to Jesus as the ultimate example of such behavior.

because to this you were called so that you may inherit a blessing.

There is some question whether "this" refers backward to the exhortation to repay evil with blessing, or forward to "that

---

[22]Verses 8 and 9, which are one sentence in the Greek text, involve another case (see 1:13; 2:18; 3:1,7) of taking a participle, and in this case several adjectives, as having the force of imperatives. See chapter 1, footnote 22.

you may inherit a blessing." The second alternative is represented by the NRSV: "It is for this that you were called — that you might inherit a blessing." The context of verses 10-12 suggests that it points backwards. Of course Peter does not mean that by repaying evil with blessing one earns this inheritance. But he does indicate what behavior those who have been blessed by God are called upon to exhibit toward others, and he implies that one may lose the inheritance by stubbornly refusing to do right.

3:10 For, "Whoever would love life and see good days must keep his tongue from evil and his lips from deceitful speech. 3:11 He must turn from evil and do good; he must seek peace and pursue it. 3:12 For the eyes of the Lord are on the righteous and his ears are open to their prayer. But the face of the Lord is against those who do evil."

Peter supports verse 9 with a citation of the Septuagint version of Psalm 34:12-16. This section of Scripture is appropriate for Peter's use in several ways. Psalm 34 as a whole is appropriate because it encourages the persecuted righteous, reminding them that "the LORD hears them; he delivers them from all their troubles" (v. 17). The references to doing good and being righteous resonate with a repeated theme in 1 Peter (see the comments at 2:14). The exhortations to control the tongue fit the immediate context and Peter's exhortation not to repay insult with insult. The opening statement concerning "Whoever would love life and see good days," while originally referring to the present life, can in the context of verse 9 emphasize the future life and good days to be inherited by those who repay evil with blessing. The final remarks that God listens to the prayers of the righteous, but is set against those who do evil, resonates with Peter's remarks about behavior and its influence on prayer in 3:7 and 4:7.

This citation brings the section 2:11–3:12 to an appropriate end.

IV. ENCOURAGEMENT TO THOSE WHO SUFFER FOR DOING GOOD (3:13–4:11)

A. DO NOT BE FRIGHTENED (3:13-17)

¹³Who is going to harm you if you are eager to do good? ¹⁴But even if you should suffer for what is right, you are blessed. "Do not fear what they fearᵃ; do not be frightened."ᵇ ¹⁵But in your hearts set apart Christ as Lord. Always be prepared to give an answer to everyone who asks you to give the reason for the hope that you have. But do this with gentleness and respect, ¹⁶keeping a clear conscience, so that those who speak maliciously against your good behavior in Christ may be ashamed of their slander. ¹⁷It is better, if it is God's will, to suffer for doing good than for doing evil.

ᵃ*14* Or *not fear their threats*   ᵇ*14* Isaiah 8:12

This paragraph and 4:12-19 are similar in their sustained focus on the persecution Peter's readers were enduring for following Christ and doing good. Both sections exhort the readers to set their course firmly on doing good and to be prepared to suffer. They are key paragraphs in the letter.

3:13 Who is going to harm you if you are eager to do good?

This is a rhetorical question with the implied answer, "no one." But how can Peter say "No one is going to harm you for doing good"? He is writing precisely because someone is harming Christians for doing good. He will later say that suffering for doing good is not to be considered strange or unusual (4:12) and that it is the experience of Christians throughout the world (5:9).

Some respond that in 3:13 Peter is speaking proverbially. According to this view, Peter intends to say that it is generally true that people will not harm others for doing good — but of course he is aware of exceptions.[23]

I am inclined to another view which holds that Peter is drawing a conclusion from the citation of Psalm 34 in verses 10-12: the Lord sees and rewards the righteous and thus no ultimate harm can come to them. This is mildly supported by the conjunction καί (*kai*) at the beginning of this verse. It is left untranslated by the NIV, but may be translated "then" or "and so." This would indicate that verse 13 is a conclusion drawn from verses 10-12.[24] Peter's point would be that no one can separate the Christian from God or take away his or her inheritance.

3:14 But even if you should suffer for what is right, you are blessed.

The statement "if you should suffer" does not call into question whether some of Peter's addressees are suffering, which is assumed throughout the book. However, the suffering envisioned by Peter is sporadic and affects different individuals in different ways and at different times. He has just said that no one can ultimately harm them for doing right. In harmony with that he now adds that in fact when they do suffer for doing right, they should consider themselves blessed. 1 Peter 4:14 makes the similar statement, "If you are insulted because of the name of Christ, you are blessed." Both echo and perhaps consciously allude to statements in the Beatitudes: "Blessed are those who are persecuted because of righteousness. . . . Blessed are you when people insult you . . . because of me" (Matt 5:10-11).

"Do not fear what they fear; do not be frightened."

These clauses are adapted from the Septuagint version of Isaiah 8:12. In the first clause Peter says literally "Do not fear

---

[23]Davids, *First Epistle*, pp. 129-130; Goppelt, *Commentary*, pp. 240-241.
[24]See Michaels, *1 Peter*, p. 185; Achtemeier, *1 Peter*, p. 229.

their fear." His unusual phraseology reflects the influence of the Isaiah passage. What he intended is probably best represented by the NIV footnote: "Do not fear their threats" (that is, "their fear" means "the fear they try to produce in you"). Peter exhorts his audience not to fear people (cf. 3:6 "do what is right and do not give way to fear"). The One whom they should fear is God (see the comments at 1:17).

3:15 But in your hearts set apart Christ as Lord.

At the end of verse 14 Peter cited Isaiah 8:12. The very next statement in the Septuagint version of Isaiah 8:13 says — in contrast to fearing men (v. 12) — to sanctify the Lord and fear him. Peter adapts this statement to his context, calling upon his readers to sanctify (ἁγιάζω, *hagiazō*, "set apart") Christ as Lord. They must not be deterred by fear of those who cause them to suffer for doing right. The one to be revered is Christ.

Always be prepared to give an answer to everyone who asks you to give the reason for the hope that you have.

In the Greek text this sentence is not a sentence, but a clause that is dependent on the exhortation to sanctify Christ as Lord. The way in which they should do that is by always being prepared to stand firm for him. They must be ready to give a defense of their actions and beliefs as followers of Christ.

It is possible that the language here suggests formal legal proceedings. This possibility is more easily seen in the NRSV rendering "make your defense to anyone who demands from you an accounting." But the language can be used, as the NIV suggests, in settings that have nothing to do with legal proceedings (e.g., 1 Cor 9:3). In either case the Christian should sanctify Christ as Lord by being ready to defend their hope in him. Peter uses the word "hope" in a way that is nearly synonymous with "faith" (cf. 1:3,13,21).

Although studying Christian apologetics is a good thing, Peter is not using "be prepared to give an answer" in the sense of "study so that you will know how to defend your beliefs." A better translation might be "be ready to give an answer." Peter uses the same word that appears in 1:5, where he speaks of a salvation "ready" to be revealed.

But do this with gentleness and respect,

Are these qualities mentioned in relationship to those who call Christians to account or in relationship to God? The word translated "respect" is the same word (*phobos*) used in verse 14 and elsewhere for "fear." It is clear in verse 14 that Christians are not to fear men. The NRSV translation "reverence" is preferable. The second word, then, seems to refer to our attitude toward God. The word πραΰτης (*praütēs*) translated "gentleness" may do the same. In some passages (e.g., Jas 3:13) the NIV translates it as "humility." However, responding to others with humility and reverence toward God would result in gentleness toward the questioner — in refusing to repay insult for insult (cf. 3:9).

3:16 keeping a clear conscience, so that those who speak maliciously against your good behavior in Christ may be ashamed of their slander.

The clause "keeping a clear conscience" gives further credence to the idea that the previous qualifications, humility and reverence, refer primarily to one's characteristics before God. There are several ways in which Christians might respond to their opponents and in so doing compromise their conscience. The immediate context suggests that they might return insult for insult (cf. 3:9) or allow themselves to be intimidated into compromising their faith (cf. 3:6,14).

If Christians stand firmly for their beliefs and respond to their opponents with humility and reverence, maintaining a good conscience, some of their opponents will recognize this and be ashamed of slandering them. This hope repeats a theme found also in 2:12 (cf. 3:1-2).

3:17 It is better, if it is God's will, to suffer for doing good than for doing evil.

This verse echoes 2:19-20 (cf. 4:15-16) where Peter tells slaves that there is no merit to bearing up well under a deserved beating. What is commendable before God is suffering for doing good. The idea that such unjust suffering could be God's will is repeated in 4:19. There is a sense, of course, in which such suffering is not what God wants, but rather the will of evil men and of their master, Satan. However, as the book of Job and other sections of Scripture indicate, God ultimately controls men and Satan. Everything he allows to happen is in some sense his will. First Peter contains several suggestions as to why God might permit unjust suffering in the lives of Christians. It proves the genuineness of their faith and purifies it like fire purifies gold (1:7). And it provides an opportunity for leading nonbelievers to faith (2:12; 3:1-2; 4:16).

B. CHRIST ALSO SUFFERED — AND WAS EXALTED (3:18-22)

[18]**For Christ died for sins once for all, the righteous for the unrighteous, to bring you to God. He was put to death in the body but made alive by the Spirit, [19]through whom[a] also he went and preached to the spirits in prison [20]who disobeyed long ago when God waited patiently in the days of Noah while the ark was being built. In it only a few people, eight in all, were saved through water, [21]and this water symbolizes baptism that now saves you also — not the removal of dirt from the body but the pledge[b] of a good conscience toward God. It saves you by the resurrection of Jesus Christ, [22]who has gone into heaven and is at God's right hand —**

with angels, authorities and powers in submission to him.

ª*18,19* Or *alive in the spirit,* *¹⁹through which*   ᵇ*21* Or *response*

This paragraph encourages us to be willing to endure unjust suffering for doing good by pointing to the example of Jesus who endured unjust suffering on our behalf. We are reminded not only that he suffered for us, but that he triumphed over death, proclaimed victory over his enemies, and was exalted to the right hand of God. We are also reminded of the commitment we made to him in baptism. Although several aspects of these verses are difficult and subject to diverse interpretations, these main thrusts of the paragraph are clear.

3:18 For Christ died for sins once for all, the righteous for the unrighteous, to bring you to God.

There is a complicated textual variant involving the words "died for sins."[25] The preferable choice is probably the one represented by the NRSV text: "Christ also suffered for sins."[26]

To a limited extent the use of the word "also" may point to Peter's use of the idea of imitating Christ's example: Christians should be willing to suffer for doing good (3:17) in imitation of Christ who "also" suffered even thought he was righteous. However, in pointing out the atoning value of Christ's suffering and saying that he suffered "once for all" Peter emphasizes unique aspects of Christ's suffering. The motivation provided here is less like that in 2:21-23 (that Christ left us an example to follow in his steps) and more like that in 2:24 (that he bore our sins so that we might die to sin and live for righteousness). Christ, the righteous one, made a once for all atonement for us, who were once unrighteous, for the purpose of bringing us to God.

---

[25]See *UBS⁴* and Metzger, *Textual Commentary,* pp. 622-623, for information and discussion.

[26]The NRSV footnote says, "Other ancient authorities read *died.*"

He was put to death in the body but made alive by the Spirit,

The interpretation and therefore translation of this part of the verse is a matter of ongoing debate. The NIV translation of the last phrase, "by the Spirit," is probably incorrect. It overrides the parallelism in the Greek text between the two halves of an "on the one hand (μέν, *men*). . . on the other (δέ, *de*)" construction (the NIV does not translate the two conjunctions). The first half says "on the one hand he was put to death in the body." In this case nearly all interpreters agree that "in the body" means something like "in the sphere of the body."[27] This makes it likely that the second clause should be understood in a parallel sense, "on the other hand he was made alive in the sphere of the spirit." The NRSV translation is probably correct: "He was put to death in the flesh, but made alive in the spirit."

There is no reason to believe that "made alive in the spirit" refers to an intermediate state between Jesus' death and resurrection. "Put to death in the flesh" unquestionably refers to Jesus' death on the cross. "Made alive in the spirit" most naturally refers to his resurrection in which he rises to life in a new plane. Compare Paul's statement concerning the resurrection of Christians: "he who raised Christ from the dead will also give life (the same verb translated 'made alive' in 1 Peter 3:18) to your mortal bodies" (Rom 8:11).

3:19 through whom also

If the NIV translation of verse 18 "by the Spirit" is incorrect, then "through whom" is also incorrect. The NRSV is probably correct in translating "in which," that is, in the sphere of the

---

[27]The grammatical explanation is that σαρκί (*sarki*, flesh) is a dative of sphere. Another possibility, with similar meaning, is a dative of reference: "he was put to death with reference to the body."

This concensus is questioned by Achtemeier, *1 Peter*, p. 250, who argues for "put to death by flesh," understanding flesh to stand for humanity.

spirit. Whatever verse 19 refers to is done after Jesus' resurrection, his being made alive in the sphere of the spirit.

he went and preached to the spirits in prison 3:20 who disobeyed long ago when God waited patiently in the days of Noah while the ark was being built.

The words of Luther concerning this text have been cited many times: "This is a strange text and certainly a more obscure passage than any other passage in the New Testament. I still do not know for sure what the apostle means."[28] I do not know for sure what the apostle means either, but I will give my opinion.

There are three major interpretations (and numerous variations which will not be described here).[29]

One view holds that Jesus went to Hades and preached to the spirits of those who had been disobedient in the days of Noah.[30] Most of those who hold this view believe that Jesus did this while his body was in the tomb. There is extensive debate about whether he offered them any opportunity for salvation.

The interpretation I have defended for the last part of verse 18 and the first few words of verse 19 suggests that Jesus' going and preaching happened after the resurrection, not during the three days in the tomb. Furthermore, Peter says that Jesus preached "to the spirits who disobeyed," not "to the spirits *of the men* who disobeyed." According to this first view, when they disobeyed they were not spirits, but men. One might expect Peter to use a construction parallel to

---

[28]As cited by Goppelt, *Commentary*, p. 255, with the note: "From the 1523 commentary, as translated in M.H. Bertram, 'Sermons on the First Epistle of St. Peter,' *Luther's Works XXX: The Catholic Epistles* (ed. J. Pelikan and W.A. Hansen; St. Louis, 1967), 113 = XII, 367 in the Weimar edition."

[29]See W.J. Dalton, *Christ's Proclamation to the Spirits; A Study of 1 Peter 3:18–4:6*, 2nd ed., Analecta Biblica 23 (Rome: Pontifical Biblical Institute, 1989), pp. 27-50.

[30]So, e.g., Goppelt, *Commentary*, pp. 255-260.

Hebrews 12:23, in which the writer speaks of the spirits of those who had died as "the spirits of righteous men."

A second view holds that by means of the Spirit Jesus preached through Noah (that is, he inspired Noah to preach) to Noah's contemporaries.[31] These men were disobedient and thus their spirits (or souls) were imprisoned after their deaths. But according to this view Jesus is said to have preached to them through Noah while they were alive.

The arguments I have used against the first view also apply to the second. Furthermore, for this view one must add not only "to the spirits *of the men* who disobeyed," but "to the spirits *now* in prison." According to this second view these spirits were neither disembodied nor in prison when Jesus preached to them through Noah.

This brings us to the third view, which is that after his resurrection Jesus preached to certain supernatural beings who had been disobedient during the times of Noah. The New Testament frequently uses the word "spirits" to refer to supernatural beings (e.g., Heb 1:14: Rev 1:4), usually evil ones (e.g., Matt 8:16; 12:45). Those who hold this view usually argue specifically that he proclaimed victory over the fallen angels of Genesis 6:1-4.[32] This story immediately precedes the story of Noah and is easily associated with it.[33]

This is, of course, to explain one obscure passage by another. The identity of the "sons of God" in Genesis 6:1-4 is itself a matter for debate. What is not debatable is that the "fallen angels" view is a plausible interpretation of Genesis 6

---

[31]This view is well defended by Wayne Grudem, *The First Epistle of Peter*, Tyndale New Testament Commentaries (Grand Rapids: Eerdmans, 1988), pp. 203-239.

[32]This view is well defended by Dalton. Grudem, *First Epistle*, p. 204, n. 5, describes it as "probably the dominant view today." My own views of the entire section 3:18-22 have been heavily influenced by the analysis of R.T. France, "Exegesis in Practice: Two Samples," in *New Testament Exegesis*, ed. I. Howard Marshall (Grand Rapids: Eerdmans, 1977), pp. 264-281.

[33]Jubilees 7:21 says their disobedience caused the flood.

and that many Jews of Peter's day and before knew about this view.[34] Furthermore, a good case can be made that Jude 6 and 2 Peter 2:4 reflect this view of Genesis 6. Both New Testament texts refer to these fallen angels as kept in eternal chains in deepest darkness until the judgment. This resonates with 1 Peter's description of them as "in prison."

Several clearly pre-Christian (found among the Dead Sea Scrolls) portions of the apocryphal Jewish document 1 Enoch are especially important for this view. 1 Enoch specifically describes the fallen angels as "spirits" (e.g., 15:4,6,8) and discusses their imprisonment in some detail. It is not, of course, necessary to believe Peter reflects the influence of 1 Enoch itself (although Jude 14-15 indicates Jude was aware of it). But 1 Enoch makes it clear that at least some Jews would use language similar to Peter's to speak about the fallen angels.

If the fallen angels view is correct, what did Jesus "preach" to these spirits? The word Peter uses (κηρύσσω, kēryssō) is usually used of preaching the gospel, but not necessarily so. In Revelation 5:2 it is used simply to mean "proclaim" and in the Septuagint it is sometimes used of bringing bad news (e.g., Jonah 1:2). The context of 1 Peter suggests a proclamation of victory over these evil spirits: this would certainly be more encouraging to the readers and fits with the declaration in verse 22 that all spiritual powers have been made subject to Christ.

To summarize the view presented here I quote France's paraphrase of this section of 1 Peter with his parenthetical insertions identifying the possible relevance of these points for Peter's audience:

> He was put to death (as you may well be), but that was only in the earthly sphere: he has been raised to new spiritual life (as you will be too, if you die for him).

---

[34]Grudem, *First Epistle*, p. 211, cites seven pertinent Jewish texts: "Josephus *Antiquities* 1:73; Philo *On the Giants* 6; *Q.Gen.* 1.92; CD 2.18; 1 Enoch 6.2,6; 106.13-14; Jubilees 5.1; 10.1-6; 2 Baruch 56.12-15."

(So death was, for Jesus, the way of achievement and victory; do not fear those who can only kill the body.) In the triumph of his resurrection he went to the fallen angels awaiting judgment in their place of confinement, and proclaimed to them the victory won by his redeeming death. (Even the most wicked of spiritual powers have had to recognize the authority of the risen Jesus; whatever the forces against you, they are not his equal). These were those spirits who rebelled against God in the days of Noah . . .[35]

In it only a few people, eight in all, were saved through water,

As France observes, "the Flood, once mentioned, becomes the basis for more teaching relevant to the encouragement of persecuted Christians. Two facts are isolated from the story: (1) that few were saved; (2) that they were saved 'through water'."[36] Peter points out that only a few were saved (Noah, his three sons, and their wives) in order to encourage the Christians of Asia Minor, who were an extreme minority in their culture.

The sense of "through water" is uncertain. The analogy of Christian baptism in verse 21 suggests "through" in the sense of "by means of." But since water was the means of destruction in the flood it seems odd to refer to Noah and his family as being saved "by means of water" (as opposed to "by means of the ark"). It may be preferable to view "through" in a local sense: Noah was saved by passing through the waters of the flood into a renewed world. The analogy with Christian baptism would then be that Christians pass through the waters of baptism into a renewed life.[37]

---

[35]France, "Exegesis," p. 277.
[36]Ibid., p. 272.
[37]See Achtemeier, *1 Peter*, pp. 265-266.

3:21 and this water symbolizes baptism that now saves you also

The grammar of this clause is notoriously difficult, although the ultimate meanings of most of the proposed solutions are similar. Peter draws an analogy between Noah and his family being saved through water and Christians being saved through the water of baptism.

France observes that some are concerned that Peter's affirmation "baptism saves you" might be taken to imply a magical view of how baptism works. His response is correct and worth citing:

> Two points may be made in this connection. Firstly, such 'realist' language concerning the effect of baptism is by no means unparalleled in the New Testament;[38] any view of baptism which finds it a rather embarrassing ceremonial extra, irrelevant to Christian salvation, is not doing justice to New Testament teaching. But, secondly, Peter is very careful to qualify his statement immediately by pointing out the true nature of baptism, involving two aspects, one negative and one positive, which between them effectively allay fears of a 'magical' view . . .[39]

The two aspects France has in mind occupy the remainder of verse 21.

— not the removal of dirt from the body

Peter's first clarifying remark indicates something he does not intend within the scope of "baptism saves you." Peter is presumably not addressing an ancient misconception of baptism: it is unlikely anyone would have thought of Christian

---

[38]At this point France's note 58 says: "See e.g. Jn. 3:5; Rom. 6:3-4; Gal. 3:27; Col. 2:12; Titus 3:5."

[39]France, "Exegesis," p. 274.

baptism as dealing with washing dirt off of the body.[40] Rather, in conjunction with the next remark, Peter's point is that the outward act of baptism does not bring salvation in and of itself; it must be combined with the right inward attitude.[41] Baptism does not operate in a magical fashion.

but the pledge of a good conscience toward God.

This is another difficult clause. The NRSV provides the main alternative: "but as an appeal to God for a good conscience." The main questions are whether the first of the two key words (ἐπερώτημα, *eperōtēma*) should be translated "pledge" or "appeal" and how the word "conscience" relates to "pledge" or "appeal." Grammatically "a good conscience" may be the object or the subject of the verbal idea contained in either "pledge" or "appeal." France and Achtemeier provide detailed discussions of the complex issues involved.[42] I am mildly inclined to agree with them that Peter intends to say baptism involves pledging a good conscience to God; that is, in baptism one makes a pledge to God to maintain a good conscience, to live a life of service to God. This understanding fits well with the overall thrust of the letter.

It saves you by the resurrection of Jesus Christ,

The power behind baptism is the power of Jesus' resurrection, symbolized in our lives as we rise from the water. Compare the similar statement in 1:3 where Peter says God "has given us new birth into a living hope through the resurrection of Jesus Christ."

---

[40]Grudem, *First Epistle*, p. 162, observes in passing that Peter's remark about removing dirt from the body implies that baptism was by immersion: "(. . . note how incongruous the mention of 'removal of dirt from the body' would be if Peter thought that only a few drops of water were sprinkled on the head)."

[41]So France, "Exegesis," p. 274; Davids, *First Epistle*, p. 144.

[42]France, "Exegesis," p. 274-275; Achtemeier, *1 Peter*, pp. 269-272.

3:22 who has gone into heaven and is at God's right hand

The reference to the resurrection brings Peter back to the subject matter of verses 18-19: the exaltation of Christ. Having been resurrected from the dead, he has proclaimed victory over his enemies and has ascended into heaven to the right hand of God. The reference to Christ being at God's right hand alludes to Psalm 110:1. The image of sitting at the right hand of a king implies honor, authority, and power.

— with angels, authorities and powers in submission to him.

The three terms used here do not in themselves refer to good or bad spiritual powers. If the spirits of verse 19 are fallen angels, then the context may indicate evil powers. "In submission" is a passive participle, which may also be translated "made subject," perhaps indicating that the angels, authorities and powers envisioned here had to be brought into submission. Peter thus reminds his readers that Christ has conquered every enemy.

1 PETER 4

C. LIVE FOR THE WILL OF GOD (4:1-6)

¹Therefore, since Christ suffered in his body, arm yourselves also with the same attitude, because he who has suffered in his body is done with sin. ²As a result, he does not live the rest of his earthly life for evil human desires, but rather for the will of God. ³For you have spent enough time in the past doing what pagans choose to do — living in debauchery, lust, drunkenness, orgies, carousing and detestable idolatry. ⁴They think it strange that you do not plunge with them into the same flood of dissipation, and they heap abuse on you. ⁵But they will have to give account to him who is ready to judge the living and the dead. ⁶For this is the reason the gospel was preached even to those who are now dead, so that they might be judged according to men in regard to the body, but live according to God in regard to the spirit.

Peter again encourages his readers to face up to persecution and continue living for God. They need to avoid falling back into their old lifestyle of sin. Their former friends will abuse them for the changes they have made, but they need to follow Christ in his willingness to suffer.

4:1 Therefore, since Christ suffered in his body, arm yourselves also with the same attitude,

The first clause is similar to 3:18, "He was put to death in the body." Peter calls upon his readers to take up the same attitude Christ had in his willingness to suffer for the will of God. "Arm yourselves" (from ὁπλίζω, *hoplizō*) uses military imagery, as Paul does in Ephesians 6:11-17 and elsewhere.

because he who has suffered in his body is done with sin.

This clause is laden with technical difficulties, for which I refer the reader to Michaels and Achtemeier.[1] On the question of the meaning of the opening conjunction ὅτι (*hoti*) I am inclined to agree with Michaels and the NIV that it should be rendered something like "because." It expresses why one should take on the attitude of Christ.[2] Against Michaels and in favor of Achtemeier I think it likely that "he who has suffered" refers in a general way to Christians and not specifically to Christ.[3] The point seems to be that when a Christian suffers for doing God's will, he or she demonstrates that they have ceased from or are done with living in violation of God's will and are ready to do God's will even if it entails suffering. The New Living Translation provides a useful paraphrase: "For if you are willing to suffer for Christ, you have decided to stop sinning."

4:2 As a result, he does not live the rest of his earthly life for evil human desires, but rather for the will of God.

The one who arms himself with the attitude of Jesus and suffers for doing the will of God has gotten out of the sinning business ("is done with sin"). The result is stated in verse 2. He will no longer live for the desires of men, but will live instead for the will of God. The next verse provides examples of the desires of men.

---

[1]Michaels, *1 Peter*, pp. 225-229; Achtemeier, *1 Peter*, pp. 277-280.

[2]The alternative is something like "namely," which makes the clause an explanation of the attitude one should have.

[3]Michaels does not wish to imply that Christ "ceased" from sin in the sense that he had been involved in it (see 1 Pet 2:22: "He committed no sin"). Rather he thinks Peter means something like that after Christ suffered he was "done with" or "finished with" the realm of sin and his bearing of it.

4:3 For you have spent enough time in the past doing what pagans choose to do

This verse is one of the clearest indications that many of these Christians were Gentiles. The word here translated "pagans" is often translated "Gentiles" (as in the NRSV translation of this verse). However, in this case it is fittingly translated "pagans" since it clearly refers to immoral and idolatrous Gentiles, not simply to the ethnic category, which would include most of Peter's audience. "Enough time" is apparently a deliberate understatement, meaning something like "more than enough" or "far too much."[4] In the past these Christians lived like pagans. Now each one must "live the rest of his earthly life" in a different lifestyle.

— living in debauchery, lust, drunkenness, orgies, carousing and detestable idolatry.

Peter's vice list resonates with other New Testament lists of pagan activities (e.g., 1 Cor 6:9-10, where Paul also reminds his readers that they had done such things in the past). It is difficult to be precise about the meaning of such words. The first two may deal primarily with sexual immorality[5] and the next three with the consumption of alcohol. The last refers to pagan worship.

4:4 They think it strange that you do not plunge with them into the same flood of dissipation, and they heap abuse on you.

"Dissipation" might be replaced by "wickedness" or "wild living."

The pagans find it unusual and disturbing that these former pagans who have become Christians have changed their

---

[4]Michaels, *1 Peter*, p. 230.

[5]It would be helpful for modern translations to quit using words like the NIV's "debauchery" or the NRSV's "licentiousness." *Merriam Webster's Collegiate Dictionary*, 10th ed., 1993, says "debauchery" means "extreme indulgence in sensuality."

lifestyles. Because Christians live a countercultural lifestyle, the pagans react against them. Peter says they "blaspheme," which may mean that they defame or slander Christians (cf. the same word in Titus 3:2) or that they blaspheme the Christians' God. The NIV translation is quite paraphrastic and provides an object ("you") that is not specified in the text. The NRSV translates more literally "and so they blaspheme."

4:5 But they will have to give account to him who is ready to judge the living and the dead.

Those pagans who currently malign Christians and their God will have to answer for it. Peter assures his readers that there will be a time of reckoning for those who are currently abusing them. They will have to give an account to God (or Christ) in the great Judgment.

4:6 For this is the reason the gospel was preached even to those who are now dead,

Although this verse is not as well known as a problem text as 3:19, it is also quite difficult. Once again there are three main lines of interpretation.[6]

One line of interpretation ties this text with the first view listed above for 3:19. According to this view, during the three days in the tomb Jesus went and preached the gospel to the spirits of the dead. The statement in 3:19 had indicated that Jesus did this for the lost of Noah's generation; 4:6 expands his proclamation to all of the dead.[7]

Those of us who reject the interpretation of 3:19 as referring to Jesus descending into Hades and preaching to the lost have no backdrop for the corresponding interpretation of 4:6. Furthermore, the context of 4:6 raises serious problems

---

[6]See the discussion in Dalton, *Proclamation*, pp. 51-60. Dalton also discusses a fourth view (the second in his list), which he says has been abandoned.

[7]Goppelt, *Commentary*, pp. 188-191.

for this interpretation. The point of verse 5 seems to be to reassure persecuted Christians that their persecutors will have to answer in the judgment for what they have done. How, in such a context, could Peter discuss a postmortem offer of salvation to the disobedient?[8]

A second line of interpretation treats the dead in 4:6 as the *spiritually* dead.[9] Against this view, it seems apparent that in verse 5 the dead are the physically dead. It is difficult to believe Peter shifts the meaning immediately without indication. Furthermore, if he is speaking of preaching to the spiritually dead why would he use the past (aorist) tense for "the gospel *was* preached" as opposed to saying "the gospel *is* preached"?[10]

The dominant view today is that the dead in 4:6 are those who were evangelized but have since died.[11] The NIV supports this interpretation by adding the word "now": "the gospel was preached even to those who are *now* dead." This view would have relevance to the context in reassuring persecuted Christians that those who have died as Christians[12] before them (perhaps some even by martyrdom) will be rewarded by God. Thus 4:5-6 assures them both of the condemnation of persecutors and of reward for Christians.

The primary problem with this view is that Peter does not say "those who are now dead," but simply "the dead." But Peter could have meant "the now dead" and this explanation seems to have less against it than the other two.

---

[8]Grudem, *First Epistle*, p. 172.

[9]R.B. Jones, "Christian Behavior under Fire (First Epistle of Peter)," *Review and Expositor* 46 (1949): 64.

[10]For these objections see Dalton, *Proclamation*, pp. 56-57.

[11]So, e.g., Michaels, *1 Peter*, pp. 235-238; Achtemeier, *1 Peter*, pp. 286-291.

[12]Michaels, *1 Peter*, pp. 239-241, argues that Peter includes the Old Testament faithful. He recognizes this strains the meaning of the verb "preach the gospel," but argues on the basis of Hebrews 4:2,6 that this verb could be used in a loose sense for the proclamation of God's will in the Old Testament period.

so that they might be judged according to men in regard to the body, but live according to God in regard to the spirit.

The contrast between "in regard to the body" and "in regard to the spirit" echoes 3:18 and probably means something similar: "in the sphere of the body" vs. "in the sphere of the spirit."

Two other contrasting pairs complicate this part of verse 6: "judged"/"live" and "according to men"/"according to God." It seems apparent that "live," when qualified by "in the sphere of the spirit," refers to eternal life. There is more debate concerning "be judged in the sphere of the body." Some take it to refer to physical death.[13] The point would be that though they receive the judgment of physical death in the sphere of the body, they rise to live in the sphere of the spirit. According to this view "according to men"/"according to God" should be translated something like "like men"/"like God."[14] They die physically like men, but they rise to live in the spirit like God.

A more common view which uses a different understanding of the prepositional phrases is that the contrast is between being judged "according to the standards of men" and living "according to the standard of God." Michaels paraphrases this interpretation as "so that even though condemned in the flesh among people generally, they might live before God in the Spirit."[15] (I would prefer "in the spirit.") This view may be a better fit in the context, since Peter has just spoken of how the pagans criticize Christians for their behavior.

Michaels provides an interesting parallel from the apocryphal Wisdom of Solomon 3:1-5 (NRSV): "But the souls of the righteous are in the hand of God, and no torment will ever touch them. In the eyes of the foolish they seemed to have died, and their departure was thought to be a disaster,

---

[13]E.g., Grudem, *First Epistle*, p. 171.
[14]Ibid., p. 171.
[15]Michaels, *1 Peter*, p. 238.

and their going from us to be their destruction; but they are at peace. For though in the sight of others they were punished, their hope is full of immortality. Having been disciplined a little, they will receive great good, because God tested them and found them worthy of himself."[16]

D. LOVE AND SERVE EACH OTHER (4:7-11)

[7]**The end of all things is near. Therefore be clear minded and self-controlled so that you can pray. [8]Above all, love each other deeply, because love covers over a multitude of sins. [9]Offer hospitality to one another without grumbling. [10]Each one should use whatever gift he has received to serve others, faithfully administering God's grace in its various forms. [11]If anyone speaks, he should do it as one speaking the very words of God. If anyone serves, he should do it with the strength God provides, so that in all things God may be praised through Jesus Christ. To him be the glory and the power for ever and ever. Amen.**

Throughout the letter Peter indicates a keen awareness that these persecuted Christians need to band together and support each other. He has already focused on their need for loving relationships in 1:22–2:5; 2:17; and 3:8. In 4:7-11 he returns to this theme.

4:7 The end of all things is near.

This statement is parallel to the statement of James that "the Lord's coming is near" (Jas 5:8). Peter shared with James, Paul, and other early Christians the opinion that the Second Coming of Jesus was at hand. Having just mentioned the coming judgment (4:5) he brings up its imminence in order to encourage his readers to faithfulness.

---

[16]Ibid., p. 239.

First Peter 4:7, James 5:8, and similar statements elsewhere raise a problem after the passing of nearly two millennia. Does the New Testament err concerning the time of the end? There are two ways to argue that it does not. First, some suggest that the New Testament writers meant only that all the conditions had been met and the Second Coming could occur at any time. In this sense the Second Coming was and is "at hand."[17] But many interpreters think Peter and others believed that the Second Coming would occur soon — not at a particular date, but in what we might call the apostolic period. A second way to handle this issue takes its clue from 2 Peter 3:3-10. There Peter addresses concerns about the delay of the Lord's coming and one of the responses he makes is that the Lord is being patient, not wanting any to perish.[18] Following this line of reasoning one might argue that the Lord has chosen to delay his coming. The idea that God may change his plans based upon the reaction of people is taught in many places in Scripture.[19]

Therefore be clear minded and self-controlled so that you can pray.

Except for the focus on prayer this statement is basically parallel to 1:13. "Be clear minded" means virtually the same thing as "Prepare your minds for action" and "be self-controlled" is the same verb in both instances. In this latter case Peter calls for clear thinking and self control because the end is near and in order to facilitate prayer. Peter's concern for prayer can also be seen in 3:7 and 12.

4:8 Above all, love each other deeply, because love covers over a multitude of sins.

Peter here returns to his emphasis on mutual love within

---

[17]Cf. Grudem, *First Epistle*, pp. 172-173.

[18]Cf. Marshall, *1 Peter*, p. 141.

[19]See especially the principles given in Jeremiah 18:7-10 and the specific example of Micah's prophecy given in Jeremiah 26:18-19.

the Christian community. Compare 1:22–2:5; 2:17; and 3:8. His statement that "love covers a multitude of sins" (cf. Jas 5:20) probably means that the one who loves another "covers" the loved one's sins in the sense that they overlook their offenses against them or the Christian community. A similar statement may be found in Proverbs 10:12: "Hatred stirs up dissension, but love covers over all wrongs."

4:9 Offer hospitality to one another without grumbling.

One way to demonstrate love is to offer hospitality, a virtue often extolled in the New Testament (e.g., Rom 12:13; Heb 13:2). Early Christian hospitality often involved hosting traveling missionaries, but Peter's "to one another" may indicate hospitality within churches. One way this would have been commonly expressed is in using one's home for the meetings of a house church. In ancient and modern times Christians need to be encouraged not to complain about the inconveniences and offenses that occur when practicing hospitality.

4:10 Each one should use whatever gift he has received to serve others, faithfully administering God's grace in its various forms.

In the Greek text this statement is a part of the sentence that began with verse 9. Practicing hospitality is one way to use the gifts God has given to serve others. In verse 11 Peter also refers to speaking the words of God and serving with the strength God provides.

Peter apparently held that every Christian receives at least one gift from God's grace to use in serving others. As Paul put it, "each man has his own gift from God; one has this gift, another has that" (1 Cor 7:7). In that context Paul had in mind his ability to live happily in celibacy. In Romans 12:6, Paul states that "We have different gifts, according to the grace given us," and then lists gifts of prophesying, serving, teaching, encouraging, giving, leading, and showing mercy.

Peter and Paul want these gifts to be used to serve others. God's gracious gifts make each Christian a steward, a manager, responsible to God for how he or she uses that which God has put in his or her care.

4:11 If anyone speaks, he should do it as one speaking the very words of God.

Those whose gift is in preaching, teaching, or prophesying should be careful to speak like they are speaking for God. Anyone who speaks for God must take their task seriously.

If anyone serves, he should do it with the strength God provides,

Achtemeier suggests that Peter chooses speaking and serving as representative of all God's gifts, which may be divided into speech and actions.[20] Just as speaking is a comprehensive term including various forms of Christian teaching, so serving is a comprehensive term including various forms of Christian ministry. Whether one speaks or serves it should be clear that the ultimate source of such activity is God. He provides the message to speak and the strength to serve.

so that in all things God may be praised through Jesus Christ.

Throughout the book Peter is concerned that Christians give praise to God (e.g., 1:3) and that they live in such a way that others will also praise him (e.g., 2:12). Their exercise of the gifts God has given them should have the same ultimate goal. Both their speaking and serving should bring praise to God.

To him be the glory and the power for ever and ever. Amen.

This doxology and amen bring this section to an end. The doxology is a natural outflow from Peter's comments about using the gifts of God's manifold grace to speak the very

---

[20]Achtemeier, *1 Peter*, p. 298.

words of God and serve with the strength God provides so that God may be praised. See the similar outburst of praise in 5:11: "To him be the power for ever and ever. Amen." Doxologies, brief outbursts of praise, are common in both Testaments. They express the purpose of all humanity, and indeed the universe, to give glory to God.

The term "amen" is commonly used to affirm the words of a doxology (e.g., Rom 11:36; Phil 4:20).

V. MORE EXHORTATIONS TO BE STEADFAST IN THE FACE OF SUFFERING (4:12–5:11)

A. REJOICE WHEN YOU SUFFER FOR CHRIST (4:12-19)

[12]Dear friends, do not be surprised at the painful trial you are suffering, as though something strange were happening to you. [13]But rejoice that you participate in the sufferings of Christ, so that you may be overjoyed when his glory is revealed. [14]If you are insulted because of the name of Christ, you are blessed, for the Spirit of glory and of God rests on you. [15]If you suffer, it should not be as a murderer or thief or any other kind of criminal, or even as a meddler. [16]However, if you suffer as a Christian, do not be ashamed, but praise God that you bear that name. [17]For it is time for judgment to begin with the family of God; and if it begins with us, what will the outcome be for those who do not obey the gospel of God? [18]And,

"If it is hard for the righteous to be saved,
    what will become of the ungodly and the sinner?"[a]

[19]So then, those who suffer according to God's will should commit themselves to their faithful Creator and continue to do good.

[a]*18* Prov. 11:31

The doxology and amen at the end of verse 11 and the "Dear friends" at the beginning of verse 12 mark 4:12ff. as a new section of the book. But most of the subject matter in 4:12–5:11 is basically the same as the preceding section 3:13–4:11. Especially similar are 4:12-19 and 3:13-17.

This section, 4:12-19, encourages Peter's audience to consider themselves blessed when they suffer for doing good. It also warns them of the judgment of God against those who do evil.

4:12 Dear friends,

Concerning this address, literally "beloved," see the comments at 2:11. In both cases it seems to indicate the beginning of a new section in the letter.

do not be surprised at the painful trial you are suffering, as though something strange were happening to you.

The verb translated "do not be surprised" (ξενίζεσθε, *xenizesthe*) is the same verb used in 4:4 of the pagan reaction to Christian behavior, "they think it strange." Peter wants to remind his readers that suffering as a Christian is not strange, but is to be expected. The idea that Christians will suffer for following Christ is common in the New Testament (see, for example, John 15:18-21; 1 Thess 3:3; 2 Tim 3:12). In 5:9 Peter will remind the Christians of Asia Minor that "your brothers throughout the world are undergoing the same kind of sufferings."

"The painful trial you are suffering" is more literally translated in the NRSV as "the fiery ordeal that is taking place among you to test you." The reference to fire and the idea of testing echo 1:6-7 where suffering is compared to testing gold by fire. The fires of persecution are a trial for their faith.

4:13 But rejoice that you participate in the sufferings of Christ,

Peter has already encouraged us to rejoice in suffering in 1:6-8. Furthermore, in 2:21-25; 3:18; and 4:1 he has appealed to Christ's sufferings as an example which we are called to follow. For the idea that following Christ in suffering entails a participation in the sufferings of Christ, see especially Philippians 2:10: "I want to know Christ and the power of his resurrection and the fellowship of sharing in his sufferings, becoming like him in his death."

so that you may be overjoyed when his glory is revealed.

The joy of Christians in the present, the focus of verse 13a, is connected to their hope of joy in the future, the focus of verse 13b. The focus on the hope of eternal life was introduced at the beginning of the book (1:3-9). Peter repeatedly urges his readers to endure present suffering in view of the hope of eternal salvation.

4:14 If you are insulted because of the name of Christ, you are blessed,

In view of the thrust of the book as a whole and its references to suffering, the word "if" in this clause should be understood to have the force of "when."[21] Several different phrases are used to express the verbal abuse these Christians are receiving because of their faith: "they accuse you of doing wrong" (2:12), "the ignorant talk of foolish men" (2:15), "they hurled their insults at him (Christ)" (2:23), "those who speak maliciously against your good behavior" (3:16). A significant element of the persecution they are enduring is verbal abuse. To be insulted "because of the name of Christ" is contextually contrasted with suffering for wrongdoing (v. 15) and is contextually parallel to "suffer as a Christian" (v. 16). The suffering that is blessed is suffering for doing good in the name of Christ. The idea that such suffering is blessed has already been expressed in 3:14. See the comments there for the parallels to Matthew 5:10-11.

---

[21]Achtememier, *1 Peter*, p. 306.

for the Spirit of glory and of God rests on you.[22]

The language of this clause alludes to the Septuagint (Greek) version of Isaiah 11:2: "And there shall rest upon him God's Spirit, the spirit of wisdom and understanding, the spirit of counsel and might, the spirit of knowledge and piety."[23] The idea of the clause is well expressed in Achtemeier's translation, "because God's glorious Spirit rests upon you."[24] God is present with Christians even in the midst of persecution.

4:15 If you suffer, it should not be as a murderer or thief or any other kind of criminal, or even as a meddler.

This verse echoes ideas found earlier in 2:19-20 and 3:17. Peter does not mean to commend justified suffering for doing wrong. "Any other kind of criminal" is a paraphrase of "an evildoer" (κακοποιός, *kakopoios*), a word which includes, but is not necessarily limited to, illegal activity. The term ἀλλο–τριεπίσκοπος (*allotriepiskopos*) translated "meddler" is quite problematic. It does not occur in all of Greek literature except here and in two later Christian authors (from the fourth and fifth centuries).[25] Our guesses about its meaning are dependent on etymology. It is a compound of a word meaning "overseer" and another word meaning "belonging to another." Several meanings are possible, including one who is supposed to oversee the goods of another, but embezzles them.[26] The most common suggestion is "busybody, meddler," one who

---

[22]As the NRSV footnotes point out, there are textual variants in this clause. The additions found in some ancient manuscripts are not very likely to be original. The two most important add "and of power" after "the Spirit of glory," and "On their part he is blasphemed, but on your part he is glorified" at the end of the verse. See Metzger, *Textual Commentary*, pp. 624-625.

[23]Translation from Achtemeier, *1 Peter*, p. 308, n. 61.

[24]Achtemeier, *1 Peter*, p. 303.

[25]See the excursus on the meaning of this word in Achtemeier, *1 Peter*, pp. 311-313.

[26]As argued by Achtemeier, *1 Peter*, pp. 311-313.

gets inappropriately involved in the business of others.[27] The main argument against this common view is that it seems unusual in a list beginning with "murderer" and "thief." A common response is that the repetition of "as" before this fourth item means something like the NIV's "even as" a meddler, indicating that meddler is separated from the rest of the list.

4:16 However, if you suffer as a Christian, do not be ashamed, but praise God that you bear that name.

As in verse 14 the use of "if" is virtually equivalent to "when." The opening clause of verse 16 is parallel to the opening clause in verse 14: "If you are insulted because of the name of Christ," although the suffering here is not necessarily limited to being insulted.

In contrast to present usage, the word "Christian" is rare in the New Testament. It appears only here and in Acts 11:26 and 26:28. Acts 11:26 implies that it was coined by non-Christians. In 26:28 it is used by Agrippa, a non-Christian; and here in 1 Peter 4:16 it may be a term of insult used against Christians. The early Christians usually referred to themselves using other terms such as "disciple" or "saint." But Acts 11:26 and 1 Peter 4:16 imply acceptance of the term "Christian," which soon became common among Christians themselves.[28]

As in verse 13 Christians are to rejoice when they suffer for Christ, so here they are to praise God. Those who ought to be ashamed are the opponents of Christians (3:16).

4:17 For it is time for judgment to begin with the family of God;

"The family of God" is more literally "the house of God." Peter uses the same word for "house" as in 2:5, "you . . . are

---

[27]So, e.g., Michaels, *1 Peter*, pp. 267-268.

[28]It is used in the early second century by Ignatius *Ephesians* 11.2; *Magnesians* 4; and elsewhere. See also the Didache 12.4.

being built into a spiritual house." As in 2:5, Peter is probably using temple imagery for the church. See the discussion at 2:5.

Most interpreters believe the context of verses 16-18 indicates that the judgment which Peter speaks of in verse 17a is the purifying effect of persecution and suffering. It is debated whether he means to say that this judgment of suffering precedes the final judgment as part of the messianic woes,[29] or perhaps that he regards such suffering as part of the final judgment itself.[30]

and if it begins with us, what will the outcome be for those who do not obey the gospel of God?

According to the prevailing view, this statement means that if Christians are dismayed at what is happening to them, they should consider the destiny of the disobedient. If they are tempted to repudiate their faith due to the suffering they are enduring, they should recognize that those who disobey God will suffer a far worse fate.

4:18 And, "If it is hard for the righteous to be saved, what will become of the ungodly and the sinner?"

In support of verse 17, Peter cites the Septuagint (Greek) version of Proverbs 11:31.[31] According to the prevailing view the point is that the fate of the disobedient will be far worse than the suffering of the righteous.

It would also seem possible to interpret verses 17-18 in another way. Perhaps Peter is not using the word "judgment" to refer to the present suffering of Christians, but is referring to the coming judgment at the end of time (as a means of inspiring Christians to remain faithful in the face of their present suffering). Peter may mean simply that the final judgment

---

[29]So Michaels, *1 Peter*, p. 270.

[30]So Achtemeier, *1 Peter*, pp. 315-316.

[31]The Hebrew text would not have suited Peter's purpose: "If the righteous receive their due on earth, how much more the ungodly and the sinner!"

is near (17a), that the first group judged will be the people of God (17a-b), that they will barely be saved (18a), and therefore that they should give great attention to avoid being among those who will be condemned (17b-18).

4:19 So then, those who suffer according to God's will should commit themselves to their faithful Creator and continue to do good.

This verse sums up the central theme of 1 Peter: Christians should continue to do good in spite of the suffering they must endure. In so doing they should follow Jesus' example: "He entrusted himself to him who judges justly" (2:23). As Creator God is interested in his creation, and he is a "faithful," trustworthy Creator.

The idea that Christian suffering is "according to God's will" echoes 3:17. See the comments there.

"Themselves" is a legitimate translation of "their souls," since in 1 Peter "soul" refers to one's life as a whole, not an immaterial spirit which separates from the body. See the comments on 1:9.

1 PETER 5

B. SHOW HUMILITY IN YOUR RELATIONSHIPS, ESPECIALLY YOU WHO SHEPHERD (5:1-5)

[1]To the elders among you, I appeal as a fellow elder, a witness of Christ's sufferings and one who also will share in the glory to be revealed: [2]Be shepherds of God's flock that is under your care, serving as overseers — not because you must, but because you are willing, as God wants you to be; not greedy for money, but eager to serve; [3]not lording it over those entrusted to you, but being examples to the flock. [4]And when the Chief Shepherd appears, you will receive the crown of glory that will never fade away.

[5]Young men, in the same way be submissive to those who are older. All of you, clothe yourselves with humility toward one another, because,

"God opposes the proud
but gives grace to the humble."[a]

[a]5 Prov. 3:34

The advice to elders and the subsequent verse about humble Christian relationships may seem out of place between two paragraphs about suffering as a Christian. However, in this situation in which Christians suffer as a persecuted minority, it is vital for them to maintain strong leadership and strong relationships with each other. The importance of how these Christians relate to each other has already been emphasized in 1:22; 2:1-5; 3:8; and 4:8-11.

5:1 To the elders among you,

The fact that verse 5 addresses those who are younger might be taken to suggest that the "elders" addressed here are not a group of leaders among the older members of the church, but rather a general address for the older members or older men. However, verses 2-3 point strongly to a group of leaders. Presumably Peter has in mind the same leadership role described as "elders" (πρεσβύτεροι, *presbyteroi*) in Acts 14:23; 20:17-18; 1 Timothy 5:17-19; Titus 1:5; and James 5:14. They were also called "bishops" (NRSV, et al.) or "overseers" (NIV) (ἐπίσκοποι, *episkopoi*), as is indicated by the interchange of the two terms in Acts 20:17,28 and Titus 1:1-7; and by the parallel between the qualifications for the elders = overseers of Titus 1:5-9 and for the overseers of 1 Timothy 3:1-7. The qualifications in 1 Timothy and Titus identify these leaders as men.

The term "elder" reflects the older age of these leaders. It was used in a similar way for leaders in various Greco-Roman groups and in Jewish communities.[1]

I appeal as a fellow elder, a witness of Christ's sufferings and one who also will share in the glory to be revealed:

"Fellow elder" translates a compound word (συμπρεσβύ– τερος, *sympresbyteros*) which Peter may have coined. It does not appear before 1 Peter and afterwards appears only in Christian literature. Peter allies himself with those he addresses. The second self-description may separate Peter from the elders in Asia Minor, if he means "eye" witness to Christ's sufferings. But Michaels may be correct in arguing that in this second description as well, Peter wishes to identify with the elders in Asia Minor.[2] If so, then "witness" (μάρτυς, *martys*) would need to be understood in a looser sense than "eye witness."[3] Peter's third

---

[1]*BAGD*, p. 700.

[2]The use of only one article before "fellow elder" and "witness" may support this idea. Michaels, *1 Peter*, p. 280.

[3]*BAGD*, p. 494, 2b.

self-description, like the first, clearly includes the elders (note his use of "also"). It echoes the reference in 4:13 to the joy Christians will receive "when his glory is revealed."

5:2 Be shepherds of God's flock that is under your care,

The imagery of the shepherd and his flock is used in the Old Testament for God and his people (e.g., Ps 23) and for Israel's leaders and Israel (e.g., Ezek 34). In the New Testament it is used by Jesus to describe himself (e.g., John 10; cf. 1 Pet 5:4) and in speaking to Peter (John 21:15-17). First Peter 5:1-3 and Acts 20:28-29 use this imagery to refer to elders and their churches. These texts use the verb ποιμάνω (*poimanō*, " to shepherd" — the NRSV "tend the flock" reflects this better than the NIV "Be shepherds"). First Peter 5:4 uses the noun ἀρχιποίμην (*archipoimēn*, "Chief Shepherd") to describe Jesus and in so doing implies that elders may be called shepherds. Ephesians 4:11 uses the noun ποίμην (*poimēn*), usually translated "pastor," in a list including apostles, prophets, evangelists, and teachers. Various aspects of shepherding are used as analogies, for example feeding may be compared to teaching, and protecting from wolves to protecting from false teachers.

God is the owner of the flock elders have been given charge of.

serving as overseers

As in the case of shepherding, the Greek text uses only a verb (ἐπισκοποῦντες, *episkopountes*), which could be literally translated "overseeing." Unfortunately, we cannot be certain whether the original text of 1 Peter had this verb. Two of our three earliest and best manuscripts omit it. However, it may have been deliberately omitted because it was perceived as redundant or because after the first century, when elders and bishops became two different offices, scribes did not believe Peter would instruct elders to do the work of bishops.[4]

---

[4]See Metzger, *Textual Commentary*, p. 625.

The noun form, overseer or bishop, is clearly used for
elders in Acts 20:28 (cf. Acts 20:17) and Titus 1:7 (cf. Titus
1:5). Although by the first half of the second century Ignatius
and others distinguish between elders and bishops, in the
New Testament there is no evidence of such a distinction.
Presumably Philippians 1:1 and 1 Timothy 3:1-2 also use the
noun form to refer to elders.

"Overseeing" highlights the elder's role as a leader for the
church.

— not because you must, but because you are willing,

Peter now uses three contrasting phrases to explain how
elders are to shepherd or oversee the flock. All three ask the
elders to do what has been (1:22; 2:1; 3:8; 4:8) and will again
(5:5) be asked of every Christian, to act out of genuine love
for other Christians.

The first contrast stresses Peter's desire that elders do
their work with a willing spirit and not begrudgingly. The sen-
timent is similar to what the author of Hebrews expresses
when he urges his readers to obey their leaders "so that their
work will be a joy, not a burden" (Heb 13:17). It is also similar
to Paul's words to Philemon when he says, "I preferred to do
nothing without your consent, in order that your good deed
might be voluntary and not something forced" (Phlm 14,
NRSV). Paul's "voluntary and not something forced" uses
prepositional phrases based on the same roots that Peter uses
in adverb form.

as God wants you to be;

There is a textual problem with the two word prepositional phrase that this clause represents. It is not in one of our
three best and earliest manuscripts as well as several others. It
may have been omitted because the Greek is somewhat difficult to understand.[5] Literally, the prepositional phrase is

---

[5]Metzger, *Textual Commentary*, pp. 625-626.

"according to God" (κατὰ θεόν, *kata theon*). As the NIV translation suggests, it probably means something like the phrase "according to the will of God" in 4:19. It is God's will that elders serve willingly and not under compulsion.

not greedy for money, but eager to serve;

This contrasting pair may presuppose that at least in some cases elders were paid for their work (cf. 1 Tim 5:17-18). It might be related to elders being in charge of church funds, with the possibility of misappropriating funds to themselves. In the second century letter of Polycarp to the Philippians (11:1-4) he refers to an elder named Valens who had apparently misappropriated church funds. The positive quality, "eager to serve," is virtually synonymous with the positive element of the previous contrast, "because you are willing."

5:3 not lording it over those entrusted to you, but being examples to the flock.

Peter's instructions that elders not act as lords over those in their charge echoes the sentiments of Jesus' instructions about leadership. In Mark 10:42-43 Jesus says, "You know that those who are regarded as rulers of the Gentiles lord it over them, and their high officials exercise authority over them. Not so with you." Peter may also have in mind a contrast with the authoritarian approach of government officials. By contrast, elders should lead the flock by example.

5:4 And when the Chief Shepherd appears, you will receive the crown of glory that will never fade away.

By calling Christ the Chief Shepherd (cf. Heb 13:20, "our Lord Jesus, that great Shepherd of the sheep") Peter identifies him as the one in charge of all the shepherds and the supreme example of what a shepherd should be.

When Jesus comes again, faithful shepherds will receive their reward. What we would call "wreathes" (made either of leaves or other vegetation, or of gold or silver), were commonly awarded to show honor, not only to athletes, but for virtually any area of endeavor (for military success, government service, making contributions as a benefactor, etc.). Peter uses the word metaphorically and in contrast to wreathes of vegetation or even precious metals which eventually rot or corrode.

5:5 Young men, in the same way be submissive to those who are older.

This instruction is parallel in structure to the instructions about submission in 2:13,17, and especially 3:1. There is some difficulty in discerning the groups addressed. The word translated "those who are older" is the same as the word translated "elders" in verse 1. The NIV translation suggests that in verse 5 Peter means not the elders *per se*, but those who are older. By the translation "young men" the NIV also suggests that both terms (younger and older) refer to men and are not gender inclusive. The NRSV, on the other hand, prefers "elders" at the end of the verse and does not refer "younger ones" only to men. In Greek the masculine plural may be used for men only or for both men and women.

It seems unlikely that Peter would switch the meaning of the word for "elder" or "older men/people" between verses 1-4 and 5. And there seems to be ample evidence in verses 2-3 for the meaning "elder" in verse 1. It is probable that by "younger ones" Peter means those — men and women — who are not elders, with an emphasis on the fact that most of them are younger than the elders.[6] Peter is exhorting the churches to submit (ὑποτάσσω, *hypotassō*) to their elders, whom he has already identified as having the responsibility of shepherding and overseeing the flock.

All of you, clothe yourselves with humility toward one another,

The elders are not to lord it over the church, and the

---

[6]See the similar use of these terms in Polycarp *Philippians* 3.3.

younger ones are to submit to the elders. All are to be characterized by humility toward each other. See the similar instructions in 3:8.

The use of clothing metaphors for taking on Christian attitudes and behaviors is common in Paul's letters (e.g., Rom 13:12; Eph 6:11; Col 3:10,12; 1 Thess 5:8).

because, "God opposes the proud but gives grace to the humble."

Peter supports his appeal for humility with a citation of Proverbs 3:34. James 4:6 cites the same text in a similar context. When we are tempted to be arrogant with one another, we need to recognize that God opposes pride and rewards humility.

C. A SUMMARIZING CALL TO SUFFER FOR CHRIST (5:6-11)

[6]Humble yourselves, therefore, under God's mighty hand, that he may lift you up in due time. [7]Cast all your anxiety on him because he cares for you. [8]Be self-controlled and alert. Your enemy the devil prowls around like a roaring lion looking for someone to devour. [9]Resist him, standing firm in the faith, because you know that your brothers throughout the world are undergoing the same kind of sufferings.

[10]And the God of all grace, who called you to his eternal glory in Christ, after you have suffered a little while, will himself restore you and make you strong, firm and steadfast. [11]To him be the power for ever and ever. Amen.

As he nears the end of the letter, Peter makes a penultimate appeal (the final appeal is in v. 12) for the Christians of Asia Minor to stand firm against Satan in the face of suffering. Many of the themes rehearsed in this section have been heard before, although a new plane is reached with the identification of Satan's role in persecution.

5:6 Humble yourselves, therefore, under God's mighty hand, that he may lift you up in due time.

Peter cited Proverbs 3:34 in verse 5 to support his appeal for Christians to show humility toward each other. Verse 6 is also based on that proverb as it encourages Christians to humble themselves before God.

In the context of 1 Peter the humbling Peter has in mind may be accepting and enduring the humiliation of rejection and persecution. Peter has repeatedly indicated that God has a purpose in allowing their situation (1:6-7; 3:17; 4:19), so that there is a sense in which their situation is an expression of God's will. They must humbly accept his will knowing that their humiliation will lead to exaltation.

The lifting up Peter has in mind is presumably the same exaltation he spoke of in 4:13 ("But rejoice that you participate in the sufferings of Christ, so that you may be overjoyed when his glory is revealed") and will speak of in 5:10 ("And after you have suffered for a little while, the God of all grace, . . . will himself restore, support, strengthen, and establish you," NRSV). All three passages have the pattern of suffering followed by exaltation. All three speak of eternal life.

5:7 Cast all your anxiety on him because he cares for you.

The verb "cast" is not actually an imperative and verse 7 is not a new sentence. "Casting" is a participle (ἐπιρίψαντες, *epiripsantes*) and verse 7 is a subordinate clause explaining part of what it means to humble oneself under God's mighty hand (v. 6). In facing their plight, these persecuted Christians should entrust themselves to God (cf. Jesus' example in 2:23), knowing that he cares for them.

5:8 Be self-controlled and alert. Your enemy the devil prowls around like a roaring lion looking for someone to devour.

Peter reiterates his exhortation to self-control (νήφω, *nēphō*; 1:13; 4:7) and adds the common New Testament exhortation to keep alert (γρεγορέω, *gregoreō*; for example,

Mark 13:35,37; 1 Cor 16:13; Col 4:2). We must do this because the devil is looking for an opportunity. Here for the first time in 1 Peter he identifies the one who incites persecution against Christians. Peter describes the devil's activities using the powerful metaphor of a lion on the prowl. He is continually looking for an opportunity to devour another Christian, to tempt another faithful man or woman into denying their savior.

5:9 Resist him, standing firm in the faith, because you know that your brothers throughout the world are undergoing the same kind of sufferings.

This verse implies that the persecutions Peter's readers are enduring are incited by the devil, so that to stand firm in their faith is to resist his attack. In this context "the faith" is not a set of doctrines, but commitment or trust (as in the NRSV translation "steadfast in your faith").

Peter reminds the Christians of Asia Minor that they are not alone in their plight. He echoes the sentiments of 4:12: "do not be surprised at the painful trial you are suffering, as though something strange were happening to you." Christians throughout the Roman world were experiencing the same kind of sufferings.

This does not imply an empire-wide official persecution. The book of Acts and Paul's letters demonstrate that various levels of persecution existed without some sort of orders from the emperor.

5:10 And the God of all grace, who called you to his eternal glory in Christ, after you have suffered a little while, will himself restore you and make you strong, firm and steadfast.

Peter's identification of God as "the God of all grace" resonates with his repeated emphasis on grace (1:2,10; 3:7; 4:10; 5:5,12). He has also previously emphasized that God called or chose his readers to inherit eternal salvation (1:2,15; 2:9; 3:9). "In Christ" perhaps should go with "who called you."

The reference to suffering "a little while" (ὀλίγον, *oligon*) echoes 1:6, "though now for a little while you may have had to suffer." In both cases the "little while" is in comparison with eternity. A lifetime of suffering is only a little while by the standard of "eternal glory."

The NRSV provides a more literal translation of the last four verbs: "[God] will restore, support, strengthen, and establish you." The NIV translation reflects the fact that the meaning of the last three verbs is heavily overlapping. The idea, of course, is that God himself will nurse them back to health and happiness when he rewards them for their suffering.

5:11 To him be the power for ever and ever. Amen.

Peter closes the body of the letter with another doxology and amen (cf. 4:11). This one is in response to verse 10 and its words about God's grace, the eternal glory he has prepared, and his coming work of restoration.

VI. CONCLUDING REMARKS (5:12-14)

[12]**With the help of Silas,**[a] **whom I regard as a faithful brother, I have written to you briefly, encouraging you and testifying that this is the true grace of God. Stand fast in it.**

[13]**She who is in Babylon, chosen together with you, sends you her greetings, and so does my son Mark.** [14]**Greet one another with a kiss of love.**

Peace to all of you who are in Christ.

[a]*12* Greek *Silvanus*, a variant of *Silas*

In Peter's day non-Christian letters were composed of a greeting, sometimes a brief prayer, the body of the letter, and concluding remarks. Peter and other early Christians followed the same pattern. Peter's concluding remarks are similar in content to those of the letters of Paul. The similarities include: references to those who would deliver the letter (Eph

6:21; Col 4:7,9), a summary of the letter's purpose (Gal 6:11-17; 1 Tim 6:20-21), greetings (Rom 16:3-16,21-23; 1 Cor 16:19-20; Phil 4:21-22; Col 4:10-15; 2 Tim 4:19-21; Titus 3:15; Phlm 23-24), what Paul calls the "holy kiss" (Rom 16:16; 1 Cor 16:20; 2 Cor 13:12; 1 Thess 5:26), and a wish for grace (in Peter's case, peace; Rom 16:20; 1 Cor 16:23; 2 Cor 13:13; Gal 6:18; Eph 6:24; Phil 4:23; Col 4:18; 1 Thess 5:28; 2 Thess 3:18; 1 Tim 6:21; 2 Tim 4:22; Titus 3:15; Phlm 25).

5:12 With the help of Silas, whom I regard as a faithful brother, I have written to you briefly,

As the NIV footnote indicates, Peter says "Silvanus." The NIV translation is based on two probable connections: 1) that this Silvanus is the same one mentioned as a cosender of 1 and 2 Thessalonians and as having worked in Corinth with Paul and Timothy (2 Cor 1:19) and 2) that that Silvanus is the Silas of Acts, a prophet (Acts 15:32) sent to Antioch from Jerusalem with the decree of Acts 15 (Acts 15:22) and then a companion of Paul on his second missionary journey (see Acts 16–18). Silvanus is a Latin name and Silas a Greek one.[7] Some suggest they are Latin and Greek versions of this man's Aramaic name. The connection of the references in 1 and 2 Thessalonians and 2 Corinthians with Paul's second missionary journey make the identification of Paul's Silvanus and Luke's Silas highly probable. It is also likely that Peter refers to the same man. In any case, Peter commends Silvanus as "a faithful brother."

"With the help of" translates a single preposition (διά, *dia*), which is often translated "through." What Peter means by this is a debated point. One possibility is that Silvanus drafted the letter for Peter. Eusebius cites a letter from Dionysius of Corinth to Rome which refers to 1 Clement (a letter written to Corinth for the Roman church by Clement of Rome) as "written *through* (using the same preposition 1 Peter uses)

---

[7]*BAGD*, p. 750.

Clement."[8] One might imagine that, like Paul (1 Cor 16:21; Gal 6:11; Col 4:18; 2 Thess 3:17), Peter used a secretary to write the book and then wrote the final few verses in his own hand. In this case he might have used the preposition "through" in a sense similar to[9] that of Dionysius, making Silvanus the person who penned the letter for Peter.

Other references suggest another meaning for "to write through someone." In Acts 15:23 the NIV's "with them they sent the following letter" translates a construction that could be translated literally as "having written through their hand." The men in mind do not seem to be the authors of the letter, but they are clearly its deliverers (see 15:22,30).[10] This usage would make Silvanus the person who carried Peter's letter to the churches.[11]

encouraging you and testifying that this is the true grace of God. Stand fast in it.

Here Peter sums up the point of his letter. Peter has written a letter of encouragement and testimony. The antecedent of "this" is perhaps the letter itself or what the letter has said about God's grace (cf. 1:2,10; 3:7; 4:10; 5:5,10). Peter wants them to endure and stand fast in God's grace, in the various aspects he has discussed: the grace of the message of the gospel (1:10), the grace of God's current work through them (4:10), the grace of suffering for Christ (2:19-20), and the grace of their future inheritance (3:7; 5:10) The entire book is an exhortation to steadfastness.

---

[8]Eusebius *Ecclesiastical History* 4.23.11.

[9]But (as Michaels, *1 Peter*, p. 307, observes) in certain respects different from.

[10]A similar use of "to write through someone" to mean "to send through someone" is probably found in the early second century letters of Ignatius (*Rom.* 10.1; *Philad.* 11.2; *Smyrn.* 12.1; *Pol.* 8.1), although it is possible that these references refer to the use of secretaries.

[11]This is the most common view. It is supported by Michaels, *1 Peter*, pp. 306-307; Achtemeier, *1 Peter*, p. 350;

5:13 She who is in Babylon, chosen together with you, sends you her greetings,

"She who is in Babylon" could conceivably refer to a woman, but the NRSV is probably correct in understanding "Your sister church in Babylon." Compare the last words of 2 John: "The children of your chosen sister send their greetings." "Chosen" echoes Peter's opening description of the Christians he writes to (1:1-2).

Babylon could refer to the well-known city in Mesopotamia or even to a Roman fortress by that name on the Nile delta in Egypt.[12] It is probably a cryptic reference to Rome, as in the book of Revelation and in the Jewish works 2 Baruch and 4 Ezra. There is early Christian tradition connecting Peter with Rome, but none connecting Peter with Mesopotamian or Egyptian Babylon.[13] The reference to Babylon presumably locates Peter in Rome when he wrote this letter.

and so does my son Mark.

"My son Mark" probably, but not necessarily, refers to John Mark of Jerusalem, whose mother's house Peter went to when the angel released him from prison in Acts 12. This John Mark traveled with Paul on the first portion of his first missionary journey, was the source of a dispute between Paul and Barnabas at the beginning of Paul's second missionary journey, and was later favorably referred to by Paul in three of his letters. Paul's references to Mark in Colossians 4:10 and Philemon 24 may place Mark in Rome. Later, 2 Timothy 4:11 summons Mark to Rome. Early church tradition, beginning in the early second century with Papias, makes a strong association between Mark's Gospel and Peter's preaching.

---

[12]The Roman fortress is referred to by Strabo *Geography* 17.1.30, and Josephus *Antiquities* 2.3.15.

[13]See the "Introduction" to this commentary, p. 17.

5:14 Greet one another with a kiss of love.

As noted in the introductory remarks to verses 12-14, the exhortation to greet each other with a kiss is found here in 1 Peter and four times in Paul, who calls it a "holy kiss." We do not know much about this practice; for example, whether it involved kissing persons of the opposite sex. By the time of Justin Martyr in the second century it was a regular part of the assembly.[14]

Peace to all of you who are in Christ.

As is pointed out in the introductory comments to verses 12-14, Paul's last words are typically a wish for grace. But in several cases Paul has an earlier wish for peace (Rom 15:33; 2 Cor 13:11; Gal 6:16; Eph 6:23; 2 Thess 3:16). Peter opens his book with a wish for grace and peace (1:2). In their beleaguered state, these Christians needed peace both between them and their opponents and as an internal quality of their hearts.

---

[14]Justin Martyr *Apology* 65: "On finishing the prayers we greet each other with a kiss."

THE BOOK OF
2 PETER

Mark C. Black

INTRODUCTION

ABOUT THIS COMMENTARY

This commentary is written for serious students of the Bible, including Bible class teachers, preachers, college students, and other motivated readers. However, it is written on a popular rather than a scholarly level, so that readers need not be familiar with Greek or scholarly methods or jargon.

The goal is to help the modern reader to hear the message of 2 Peter as its first readers heard it. Our assumption is that we must know what it *meant* before we can know what it *means*. Peter wrote for a particular group of Christians facing a particular set of problems. The letter was therefore not written *to* us (although we believe that it was written *for* us). To be faithful to Peter's intent, we must attempt to place ourselves in the shoes of the earliest readers.

This is a difficult task for a couple of reasons. First, this "book" of the New Testament is a letter. This means we are reading someone else's mail. The problem is that both Peter and his readers knew the situation, so that Peter only makes allusions to what was going on. For example, we would like to know much more about the false teachers. However, Peter had no need to discuss in detail what both he and his readers already know. We are left to read between the lines in order to reconstruct the situation. Second, we are dealing with literature written in an ancient language to an ancient culture. They had a very different worldview, lived very different lifestyles, and practiced very different customs from those with which we are familiar.

Our task is therefore difficult, but it is not hopeless. We will never grasp the details of this letter exactly as the first readers did, but we can have confidence that we are understanding the larger picture. Greek scholars, historians, specialists in ancient Jewish and Christian literature, and others have spent countless hours studying this and other ancient documents. We are fortunate to stand on their shoulders.

Finally, we must mention the nature of this letter. Many dislike it because it is largely negative. After all, it is Peter's scathing denunciation of false teachers. Everyone prefers the message of grace to the message of judgment. However, it is sometimes necessary to expose error, even if the task is not enjoyable. This letter ought to remind Christians of the importance of guarding the essential doctrines of the Christian faith. As Peter makes painfully clear, bad doctrine leads to bad living, which leads to sure judgment. Christians must never shrink from the unpleasant task of fighting heresy.

The reader will quickly discover that I am greatly indebted to the fine commentaries of Douglas J. Moo and especially Richard Bauckham.[1] Moo offers excellent comments from an evangelical perspective. Bauckham's detailed discussion of linguistic, historical, and literary matters is without equal. The reader is referred to his commentary in numerous footnotes simply because his discussion is the most thorough available.

AUTHORSHIP AND DATE

Second Peter claims to have been written by Simon Peter, the apostle of Jesus (1:1) and eyewitness to his transfiguration (1:16-18). Since he writes of his approaching death (1:14-15), Peter must have written this letter by the mid-60s of the first

---

[1]Douglas J. Moo, *2 Peter and Jude,* The NIV Application Commentary (Grand Rapids: Zondervan, 1996); Richard Bauckham, *Jude, 2 Peter,* Word Biblical Commentary (Waco, TX: Word, 1983).

century A.D. (The tradition that Peter was martyred in Rome under the emperor Nero is probably reliable.[2])

A large number of modern scholars, however, are convinced that Peter could not have written this letter. In fact, this New Testament writing more than all others is believed to be pseudonymous (written under a false name). A number of reasons are given for this belief.

First, there is the language and style of the original Greek. Second Peter is written in elaborate Greek, often using rare and poetic terminology. Many believe that a Galilean Jew could not have written in this style. More significantly, 2 Peter is very much unlike 1 Peter. Most argue that the writer who wrote 1 Peter could not have written this letter. In response it must be admitted that this is an argument of some weight. However, conservative scholars are not convinced. First, no one can really know what Peter could and could not have written at different times in life and to different audiences. The style argument always involves considerable subjectivity. Second, many conservative commentators admit that the style of 2 Peter disallows thinking that Peter wrote it himself. They suggest that an amanuensis probably wrote the letter for Peter, as Silvanus may have done in 1 Peter (5:12). A trusted "secretary" may well have written Peter's thoughts in a different style from that of Peter.

A second argument against Petrine authorship is that even some of the early Christians had their doubts about this letter. The evidence is quite complex and difficult to analyze, but a few facts are fairly clear.[3] Origen (3rd century) notes that 2 Peter was a disputed letter, although he believes that Peter wrote it. Eusebius (4th century) rejects its authenticity, although he suggests that the majority accepted it. Jerome (end of 4th century) writes that many rejected it because it

---

[2]1 Clement 5–6.

[3]See Donald Guthrie, *New Testament Introduction,* 3rd revised edition (Downers Grove, IL: InterVarsity Press, 1970), pp. 814-820.

was so unlike 1 Peter; yet he contends that Peter probably used two different amanuenses (secretaries). In response, it must again be granted that this is a substantive claim. More than any other New Testament book, 2 Peter was late in being universally accepted. However, evangelical scholars underscore the fact that it *was* accepted; and it was accepted at a time when a number of works falsely attributed to Peter were being rejected. The evidence from the early church is not unanimous, but it is clearly *for* the authenticity of 2 Peter.

A third argument for the pseudonymity of 2 Peter concerns the time references regarding the false teachers. At times the writer speaks of false teachers who *will* come, but at other times he makes it clear that they are already present. The argument is that the actual writer attempts to write as if Peter is predicting the future. In reality he betrays the fact that he is actually living during the times of the false teachers. In response, conservatives note that there are many possible reasons for the changing tenses. The possibility that the pseudonymous writer forgot to continue his fiction is not the most likely. Perhaps the false teachers had not arrived yet but were known because they were already present in other locations. The full discussion is found in the comments on 2:1.

Fourth, many think that the inference in 3:16 that Paul's letters are "Scripture" betrays a late date. Paul's letters, it is argued, were not considered Scripture until at least the late first century. Those who accept Petrine authorship must admit that Peter's words are somewhat surprising. However, it cannot be ruled out that the written words of one regarded as an inspired apostle would be called Scripture. Scholars are often too sure that they know what early Christians could and could not think.

Fifth, many who deny that Peter wrote this letter do so on the basis that it is a "testament," a final address of a leader before his death to the group which reveres him (see comments on 1:11). Most often, a testament was written well after the death of the hero whose name is attached to it, and it addressed the needs of the later generation.[4] Many believe therefore that someone wrote this testament in Peter's name in order to lend his authority to the crisis provoked by the false teachers. Conservatives have responded that there are certainly some elements of the testament genre in 2 Peter, but that these elements do not make 2 Peter a testament like others. Furthermore, testaments need not be pseudonymous. Peter certainly could have written this way at the end of his life.

Sixth, many scholars reject 2 Peter on the basis of the false teaching it opposes. Many think that the heresy is Gnosticism, which developed in the second century. However, while there are minor similarities to that heresy, there is nothing in 2 Peter that would identify the false teachers as second-century Gnostics. The sort of false teaching in 2 Peter is already seen in Paul's letters.[5]

Finally, some also argue that the apostle Peter would not have borrowed from the letter of Jude (see section on "Relation to Jude"). However, this argument is really quite weak. It is not clear why Peter would not have borrowed useful material from another source. Neither is it certain that Peter borrowed from Jude. Jude may have borrowed from Peter, or both may have borrowed from another source, whether oral or written.

In the final analysis, most conservative scholars argue that the apostle Peter wrote 2 Peter.[6] They know that this can never be proven and that the decision is in part based on faith and tradition. Nonconservative scholars make significant arguments against Petrine authorship, but they wrongly claim that they have proven that Peter did not write this letter. We find their arguments weighty but not conclusive. In this commentary we will assume that Peter wrote 2 Peter.

---

[4]See the discussion in Moo, *2 Peter*, p. 64.

[5]See the discussion in the "Occasion" section below.

[6]It should probably be noted that the teachings of 2 Peter are quite orthodox. If someone wrote in Peter's name, it was not in order to advance some new and unusual teaching, as is often the case with pseudonymous writings.

OCCASION

Peter wrote to a specific church (or group of churches) facing specific problems, namely the coming of false teachers. Second Peter may have been written to the same churches as 1 Peter (churches in Asia Minor, according to 1:1), since 2 Peter mentions an earlier letter to this group (3:1). However, the fact that he may have written letters to other churches means that we cannot be sure.

Peter wrote this letter primarily because false teachers were 1) denying the Second Coming of Jesus, and 2) living without moral restraint and encouraging others to do so. Peter writes that they denied the teachings of prophets and apostles and that they arrogantly slandered spiritual beings. They denied the Second Coming, arguing that the world was simply continuing on its course as it had since the creation.

Their belief that there would be no Second Coming (and therefore no final judgment) led these false teachers into ungodly lifestyles. They willfully satisfied their sinful desires, including greed, sexual immorality, and gluttony. They encouraged others to follow their sinful examples, especially recent converts who were just escaping these very sins.

Readers of 2 Peter would like to know more about these teachers of error. There is much that we do not know, because of the nature of a letter. (Both author and recipients knew the situation, so there was no need to rehearse the details.) It would be helpful to know more precisely the identity of the false teachers, their background, their practices, and their teaching. This lack of information has led scholars to speculate regarding the identity of the troublemakers. Many have theorized that they were Gnostics, a group of second-century heretics who argued that knowledge was the key to salvation. They believed in a strict dualism between the spiritual and the physical worlds. Therefore they did not believe that Christ was actually human. They also tended to discount the importance of sins involving the body, such as sexual sin. The body, they claimed, belonged to the evil physical world that was created by an inferior god.

There is no evidence in 2 Peter that the false teachers were Gnostics since there is not a trace of the developed Gnostic systems of the second century. Furthermore, all of the teachings which Peter attacked are also found in Paul's letters. For example, in 1 Corinthians Paul writes against some who deny the resurrection (15:12-34) and others who argue for the right to engage in sexual sin (5:1-2; 6:12-20). The most that can be said is that 2 Peter's antagonists may have been the predecessors of what would later be called Gnostics.

A better and more cautious approach is to call these false teachers simply libertines. Their libertine approach seems to have sprung from their (false) understanding of grace and their denial of the judgment at the Second Coming of Jesus.

Another reason Peter wrote 2 Peter is that he was nearing the end of his life. This may have been his last opportunity to offer his teachings concerning sin, judgment, and false teachers. This was especially important because he was an eyewitness to the life, death, and resurrection of Jesus. As an apostle, it was his responsibility to testify to the truth about Jesus and to destroy the efforts of the false teachers.

RELATION TO JUDE

Portions of 2 Peter and Jude are remarkably similar. This applies not only to their contents but also to their order. They use the same examples of destruction for sinfulness: evil angels cast into hell and the judgment against Sodom and Gomorrah. They use similar metaphors, such as clouds or mists driven by a storm. They speak in the same way of the false teachers, including their slander of celestial beings and their following the way of Balaam. They speak of their opponents as "scoffers" and their readers as "friends."

Most scholars think that the resemblance between the two letters is simply too close to be coincidental. It is remotely possible that both may be relying on an *oral* body of teaching against false teachers. However, it is likely that there is a literary dependence between the two letters. It could be that Peter has used Jude, Jude has used Peter, or that both have used another written source. Very few argue for a third (unknown) source used by both, since this only compounds the problem. Most think that Peter used Jude, and they may be correct. It does seem more plausible that Peter adapted and expanded Jude than that Jude used only a portion of 2 Peter and added very little to it.

However, the fact is that all theories about the literary relationship are conjectural. Fortunately, we need not know the direction of influence in order to interpret the letter. It is obvious that both writers are facing similar problems. Their churches were facing so-called Christian teachers who not only taught false doctrine but lived ungodly lives.

OUTLINE

I. INTRODUCTION — 1:1-15
   A. Salutation and Greeting — 1:1-2
   B. Preface: Exhortation to Godly Living — 1:3-11
   C. Occasion: The Approaching Death of Peter — 1:12-15

II. BODY OF LETTER — 1:16–3:13
   A. Reasons for Believing in Christ's Return — 1:16-21
      1. Peter's Eyewitness Testimony — 1:16-18
      2. The Sure Prophetic Word — 1:19-21
   B. Warning against False Teachers — 2:1-22
      1. The Coming of False Teachers — 2:1-3
      2. The Condemnation of False Teachers — 2:4-10a
      3. The Sins of the False Teachers — 2:10b-16
      4. The Future Suffering of the False Teachers — 2:17-22
   C. The Necessity of Believing in Christ's Return — 3:1-13
      1. The Content of the False Teaching — 3:1-7
      2. The Sure Return of Christ — 3:8-10
      3. Christian Living in Light of Christ's Return — 3:11-13

III. FINAL EXHORTATIONS — 3:14-18

BIBLIOGRAPHY
2 PETER

Bauckham, Richard. *Jude, 2 Peter.* Word Biblical Commentary. Waco, TX: Word, 1983.

Green, Michael. *The Second General Epistle of Peter and the General Epistle of Jude.* Tyndale New Testament Commentary. Grand Rapids: Eerdmans, 1968.

Hillyer, Norman. *1 and 2 Peter, Jude.* New International Biblical Commentary. Peabody, MA: Hendrickson, 1992.

Kelly, J.N.D. *A Commentary on the Epistles of Peter and of Jude.* Harper's New Testament Commentary. San Francisco: Harper & Row, 1969.

Mayor, Joseph B. *The Epistle of St. Jude and the Second Epistle of St. Peter: Greek Text with Introduction, Notes, and Comments.* Grand Rapids: Baker, 1979 (orig. 1907).

Moo, Douglas J. *2 Peter and Jude.* The NIV Application Commentary. Grand Rapids: Zondervan, 1996.

Neyrey, Jerome H. *2 Peter, Jude: A New Translation with Introduction and Commentary.* Anchor Bible. New York: Doubleday, 1993.

2 PETER 1

I. INTRODUCTION (1:1-15)

A. SALUTATION AND GREETING (1:1-2)

¹Simon Peter, a servant and apostle of Jesus Christ,
To those who through the righteousness of our God and Savior Jesus Christ have received a faith as precious as ours:
²Grace and peace be yours in abundance through the knowledge of God and of Jesus our Lord.

1:1 Simon Peter, a servant and apostle of Jesus Christ,

This is a standard beginning for Greek letters in general and for early Christian letters in particular. Unlike modern English letters, authors of Greek letters would first state their names and then further identify themselves. They would then state the name(s) of the recipient(s), followed often by some sort of thanksgiving or blessing to or from the gods. On the question of authorship, see the introduction above. The letter claims to have been written by Peter, and we accept this claim in this commentary.

This document is a letter, written for a specific group of Christians (although Peter probably intended that it be copied and read by others). However, this letter also includes many characteristics of the type of literature known as a "testament." Testaments were usually written or narrated at the end of the lives of famous heroes of the faith. They included such elements as 1) the mention of the imminent death of the speaker/writer, 2) ethical instructions to the family or group, and 3) predictions of the future for that group.

The NIV translation "Simon Peter" obscures the fact that the Greek has the more primitive and Jewish "Simeon" (Συμεών), which Peter would have been called by his Aramaic-speaking friends. Only in Acts 15:14 in the New Testament is this form used instead of Simon (Σίμων), when James, the brother of Jesus, uses it. The name Peter is actually his nickname, given to him by Jesus (Mark 3:16; John 1:42). Since Peter means "rock," Jesus may have been looking ahead to Peter's later role as one of the pillars of the early church.[1]

Peter's descriptions of himself show him to be one under authority and having authority. The term "servant" (δοῦλος, *doulos*) refers not simply to one who serves but to a slave, one whose will is completely subject to another. Peter therefore reminds his readers that his life has been completely given over to Christ. Perhaps his readers are to remember that his life has been one of persecution, hardship, and courage. He has earned the right to be heard. At the same time, he does not hesitate to remind them that as Christians, they have an obligation to accept his teaching. He is a chosen apostle of Jesus, and any readers who may be listening to the false teachers need to be reminded of this fact. The term "apostle" (ἀπόστολος, *apostolos*) in this context refers to the authoritative role first shared by the twelve and later expanded to include other men who were witnesses to Jesus' resurrection.[2] In Ephesians 2:20 Paul mentions apostles first in his ordered list of leaders in the early church. They were the guarantors of the message of Jesus during the earliest days of the church, and their words in writing (in the New Testament) function in the same way today.

---

[1]In Matthew 16:18, Jesus makes a play on this name, tying it to Peter's foundational confession of Jesus as Messiah, Son of God.

[2]1 Corinthians 15:5-9 makes a distinction between "the twelve" and other apostles. Among the latter are at least Barnabas (Acts 14:4,14), James the Lord's brother (Galatians 1:19), and, of course, Paul. The term "apostle" can also be used in the more general sense of missionary, as it seems to be used in 2 Corinthians 8:23, Philippians 2:25, and perhaps Romans 16:7.

To those who through the righteousness of our God and Savior Jesus Christ have received a faith as precious as ours:

Peter does not specify the church(es) to whom he is writing his letter. Chapter 3 relates that these believers had collected some of the letters of Paul. Therefore the best guess is that Peter is writing to Christians in Galatia, Asia Minor, Greece, or perhaps Italy. Here, however, Peter only identifies them as those who "have received a faith as precious as ours." The term "ours" probably refers to the apostles, since Peter has just identified himself as an apostle. These Christians, who were *not* eyewitnesses of Jesus (see 1:16), had faith that was in no sense inferior to that of the apostles themselves. (For a similar thought, see John 20:29.)

The way in which Peter describes how these readers became Christians puts all the emphasis on God's activity rather than on human activity. It was "the righteousness of our God and Savior Jesus Christ" that led them to faith. While the term "righteousness" (δικαιοσύνη, *dikaiosynē*) can mean justice, fairness, or justification, the term here most likely echoes its common New Testament meaning. It refers to the characteristic of God which caused him to offer and accept the sacrifice of Jesus on the cross.

The phrase "our God and Savior Jesus Christ" is unusual in that it seems to call Jesus "our God and Savior." The wording in Greek makes it all but certain that this is one of those rare passages in the New Testament where Jesus is explicitly called "God."[3]

When Peter writes that his readers have "received" their faith, he may imply that faith is something Christians receive as a gift, just as grace is a gift. However, it is more likely that Peter is here simply reminding these Christians that they

---

[3]Of course, it is implied in almost every NT book that Jesus is God. However, it is expressed that way in only a few texts, such as Titus 2:13 and John 1:1.

"received" faith when they accepted or believed the message about Jesus. In either case, the emphasis is on what God has done rather than what the believers have done. This is underscored by Peter's assertion that his readers' faith is "as precious as ours." As stated above, Peter means that the faith of these Gentile Christians is no less valid and valuable than that of the apostles themselves. These Christians received salvation the same way that all Christians do. They put their trust in the righteous act of God, the death of Jesus Christ.

1:2 Grace and peace be yours in abundance through the knowledge of God and of Jesus our Lord.

Peter's greeting, a prayer that his readers might continue to enjoy grace and peace, was very common among the early Christians. Peter wrote much the same thing in 1 Peter 1:2, and Paul uses these two terms in the greetings of all his letters. "Grace" (χάρις, *charis*) would include all of God's gifts which issue from his grace, including, among others, the fruit of the Spirit (Gal 5:22-23) and special gifts of ministry, prophecy, and the like (Rom 12:3-8). "Peace" (εἰρήνη, *eirēnē*) was the common Jewish greeting, expressing the desire that its recipient experience peace within and without, especially in relationships with God and with other people.

The reference to "knowledge" already anticipates the major reason for Peter's writing. The false teachers had a knowledge problem — they denied the truth concerning Jesus' Second Coming. This errant knowledge then had disastrous consequences for their lives. They were completely overcome by sin (see chapter 2), thus destroying their relationship with Christ. Here, as elsewhere in Scripture, knowledge is not simply an intellectual matter but also a relational one. The false teachers did not truly "know" God. Peter's prayer, then, is that his readers will have the abundant grace and peace that comes from knowing God and knowing the truth about God and about Jesus our Lord.

Our modern (better, postmodern) world needs to hear Peter's emphasis on knowledge every bit as much as did the original readers. A focus on the truth about God apart from a relationship with God will leave the Christian powerless to defeat sin. Similarly, an emphasis on the relationship without a deep concern for doctrinal truth will lead to sins which are the result of wrong thinking. As 2 Peter makes clear, Christians must get beyond just the basic facts if they expect to mature.

B. PREFACE: EXHORTATION TO GODLY LIVING (1:3-11)

[3]His divine power has given us everything we need for life and godliness through our knowledge of him who called us by his own glory and goodness. [4]Through these he has given us his very great and precious promises, so that through them you may participate in the divine nature and escape the corruption in the world caused by evil desires.

[5]For this very reason, make every effort to add to your faith goodness; and to goodness, knowledge; [6]and to knowledge, self-control; and to self-control, perseverance; and to perseverance, godliness; [7]and to godliness, brotherly kindness; and to brotherly kindness, love. [8]For if you possess these qualities in increasing measure, they will keep you from being ineffective and unproductive in your knowledge of our Lord Jesus Christ. [9]But if anyone does not have them, he is nearsighted and blind, and has forgotten that he has been cleansed from his past sins.

[10]Therefore, my brothers, be all the more eager to make your calling and election sure. For if you do these things, you will never fall, [11]and you will receive a rich welcome into the eternal kingdom of our Lord and Savior Jesus Christ.

1:3 His divine power has given us everything we need for life and godliness through our knowledge of him

This section is a preface to the main body of the letter, encouraging holy living among Peter's readers. He clearly believes that Christians must put forth effort in order to live acceptably, although he believes that everything needed for success in that effort has been provided by Christ. The result will be "life and godliness," which may be taken as a single idea or as two related ideas. "A godly life" may be the best translation. The Greek term translated "godliness" (εὐσεβεία, *eusebeia*) was well known in the Greek world, meaning "piety," doing what the gods desired for one to do. In the New Testament it takes on a more ethical sense of holy living.[4]

It is difficult to know just what Peter has in mind when he relates that "divine power" has supplied his readers' needs through their "knowledge." It does seem that the referent of "his" and "him" is Christ, the closest antecedent (in verse 2). Peter may be teaching that Christ continually provides to Christians the power to defeat sin and live godly lives (through the Holy Spirit). However, he may mean that the knowledge Christians have of Jesus' death and resurrection on their behalf in itself gives them power to live as Christians. (Both possibilities express truths — we simply do not know which Peter intended.) In either case, Christians have this ability through knowledge. Christian knowledge of Christ implies both content (death, resurrection, Second Coming, etc.) and relationship (personally knowing Christ, reception of his Spirit), so that our knowledge of Jesus' life gives us courage to live as he did, and he continues to support us in various ways as our living Lord.

who called us by his own glory and goodness.

Peter often uses terms in pairs, such as grace and peace,

----

[4]It occurs four times in this section of 2 Peter, ten times in 1 and 2 Timothy and Titus, and once in Acts.

life and godliness, and here "glory and goodness." Peter is probably looking back to the life, death, and resurrection of Jesus as he writes these words. Jesus' glory (δόξα, *doxa*) is his reflection of God's presence, and his goodness (ἀρετή, *aretē*) refers to his moral character.

Peter includes himself when he writes that Jesus "called us." The reader is tempted to look back to the incident recorded in Luke 5, where Peter clearly recognized Jesus' glory and goodness and then asked Jesus to leave because of his (Peter's) sinfulness. In that scene Peter was explicitly called to follow Jesus. But in what sense were the readers of this letter "called" by Jesus? Theologians throughout the centuries have debated this question, and it must suffice here to make two brief comments. First, the expression, being "called by God" (1 Pet 1:15; 2:9; Rom 1:7; 8:28; and others), is common in the New Testament and surely means more than simply that Christians have heard the gospel message. Those who are Christians are in some sense specially chosen by God. Second, just as common in the New Testament is the teaching that the gospel is for all (Acts 10:34-35), that God does not wish for any to perish (as taught in 3:9 of this letter!), and that human failure to respond to Christ is fully the responsibility of those who reject him (Acts 17:30; Matt 13:1-9,18-23). The call to repent and believe presupposes the ability of its hearers to do so.

1:4 Through these he has given us his very great and precious promises,

Peter is probably still thinking of Christ's "glory and goodness" when he tells his readers that it is "through these" that they have been given "his very great and precious promises." In light of the next clause in the sentence, the "promises" of Jesus must include his Second Coming and the resurrection of believers. They may also include his guidance and the gift of the Holy Spirit.

so that through them you may participate in the divine nature and escape the corruption in the world caused by evil desires.

The statement that these promises allow believers to "participate in the divine nature" has caused much discussion among interpreters. The phrase, "participating in the divine nature," could mean many different things, including becoming like God in his very essence. But there is no support for this understanding anywhere in this letter (or in the Bible, for that matter!). Many therefore believe that Peter is looking to the future resurrection of believers, when they will be like God in that they will have "put on immortality," to use Paul's words (1 Cor 15:53; see also 1 John 3:2). However, the context here demands a more immediate meaning, suggesting that in some way Christians become like God even in this life so that they may resist evil desires. Peter may be thinking that Christians "participate" with God through the indwelling of the Holy Spirit. However, the Holy Spirit is not mentioned here. The better opinion is that Christians are able to participate in the divine nature by being holy, as God is holy. That is, the Christian is in an important sense like God when he or she adds to faith goodness, knowledge, self-control, and the other attributes mentioned in verses 5-7. These signs of a godly life grow out of several factors, including God's help (through the Holy Spirit), the knowledge of the cleansing from past sins (verse 9), and personal effort (verse 5).

The "corruption in the world caused by its evil desires" is one of Peter's primary concerns in this letter. In chapter 2 he will severely criticize some who call themselves Christians, and there, as in these verses, he will underline the clear connection between wrong thinking (lack of knowledge) and wrong living. The false teachers' heresies have led them into greed and shameful ways. It is for this reason that Peter continuously reminds his readers that knowing the truth about Jesus, including his promises, is their best defense against being destroyed by sin.

1:5 For this very reason, make every effort to add to your faith goodness;

The phrase, "for this very reason," looks back to the whole of verses 3-4. The provisions and promises given freely by Christ demand that Christians do their part to ensure they do not lose those blessings. They must put forth the effort to supplement their faith with the virtues listed in verses 5-7. The list might first appear to demand a stair step approach to Christian virtues, so that one must take them in order and master one before moving to the next. Such an understanding, however, probably overextends the meaning of this common rhetorical device. While the first and last (faith and love) must begin and end the list, the others may not necessarily build on each other (as those in Romans 5:3-5 do). Peter is simply drawing attention to the importance of these interrelated characteristics of holy living.

The terms translated "make every effort" underscore just how hard Christians must work in order to be welcomed "into the eternal kingdom of our Lord" (v. 11). It must be noted that Peter nowhere makes salvation dependent on human effort — salvation is a gift, a "calling and election" (v. 10). However, those who truly understand and appreciate the gift will put forth the effort to let God work on them and through them. The idea is much like that of Paul who tells his readers to "run in such a way as to get the prize" (1 Cor 9:24), and to "work out your own salvation in fear and trembling, for it is God who works in you to will and to act according to his good purpose" (Phil 2:12-13). Through Jesus God saves and empowers, but Christians must allow him to do so by putting forth effort.

Lists of virtues similar to this one (as well as lists of vices) were common during the early Christian period. Well known are those in the New Testament: Romans 5:3-5; 2 Corinthians 6:4-7; 8:7; Galatians 5:22-23; Philippians 4:8; 2 Timothy 3:10-11; Titus 2:2; 1 Peter 3:8; and Revelation 2:19. Abundant examples may also be found in other early Christian literature, in Hellenistic Jewish writings, and among philosophical writings, especially those of Stoics. This list in 2 Peter is unusual among New Testament writings in that the virtues are arranged in a successive order, each being added to the one before. Only Romans 5:3-5 has a similar pattern. Some have also argued that the list here more closely resembles the philosophical lists, since it uses the terms "virtue," "self-control," and "godliness."[5]

The virtues that Peter lists, with two exceptions (faith and love), are virtues which were often praised by Hellenistic philosophers. Of course, it is only reasonable that Peter would preach the gospel in terms with which his readers would have been familiar. However, "faith" and "love" are specifically Christian in their content, and they imply a Christian content for each item in the list.

The first term is the foundation of Christian life, "faith" (πίστις, *pistis*, often translated "belief"). Like the other virtues, this one is undefined by Peter, since he assumes that his readers know its meaning. It is the trusting relationship grounded in the believer's knowledge of the life, death, and resurrection of Jesus.

"Goodness" translates the term *aretē*, a very important term in Peter's day. Among the philosophers, it meant "virtue," a characteristic of those who lived a life of integrity, based strictly on reason. The Christian understanding of the term, however, was linked to the character of God. Verse 3 has already mentioned the glory and "goodness" of Christ, pointing Peter's readers to the highest standard of moral excellence.

and to goodness, knowledge;

"Knowledge" (γνῶσις, *gnōsis*) was already in the first century a loaded term among Christians, used by some to claim

---

[5]See the comments of Bauckham, *2 Peter*, pp. 174-176, and the bibliography there.

superiority over others. Paul writes that, "Knowledge puffs up, but love builds up" (1 Cor 8:1). He also writes of "what is falsely called knowledge," referring to wild speculations about spiritual beings (1 Tim 6:20). However, the term is here used in a very positive sense, as it was more normally used in the New Testament. It refers not to the initial knowledge about Jesus' death and resurrection (a different word is used in verses 2-3). It is best understood as the deeper matters of the faith ("solid food" as opposed to "milk," as in 1 Corinthians 3:2) or even as the ability to discern God's will (see Rom 12:2; Phil 1:9-10).

1:6 and to knowledge, self-control;

"Self-control" (ἐγκράτεια, *enkrateia*) is very common in ethical lists, both Christian and philosophical. It was one of the highest ideals of Stoicism, signifying the ability to control one's emotions, to be indifferent to matters outside one's control, and thus to be one's own master. Early Christians such as Peter used it in contexts such as this one, in which the doctrine of Christian freedom was being used to justify moral permissiveness. Paul's use of the term in Galatians 5:23 provides an interesting parallel.

and to self-control, perseverance;

"Perseverance" (ὑπομονή, *hypomonē*) is found in many of the New Testament lists of Christian characteristics. The term may also be translated "steadfastness" or "endurance" and refers to the ability to withstand temptation, hardship, or persecution. For the Christian the basis of perseverance was not personal strength but trust and hope in the Lord.

and to perseverance, godliness;

Peter has already used the term "godliness" (*eusebeia*) once (verse 3) where it functioned as a general term roughly equivalent to "holy living." It may be added here that the term refers not only to behavior but also to a person's attitude toward God. It was common among pagans to speak of the need for "piety," that is, doing the right things out of a proper respect for the gods. Christian godliness refers to holy living out of respect for a holy God.[6]

1:7 and to godliness, brotherly kindness;

"Brotherly kindness" translates the term φιλαδελφία (*philadelphia*). Since the next virtue is "love," we must make a distinction between this "love of brother" and *agapē*.[7] "Brotherly kindness" in non-Christian literature referred to the natural affection between family members. In Christian contexts, however, it speaks of the tender feelings and loving actions among believers. Jesus spoke of the ties among his followers that were even stronger than biological family relationships (Luke 18:29-30). It is this love for fellow Christians that Peter mentions here.

and to brotherly kindness, love.

"Love" (ἀγάπη, *agapē*) is the supreme Christian virtue (see 1 Cor 13) and is therefore mentioned last. It may be that Peter wants the reader to understand that all of the others are encompassed in (or must be understood in light of) this one, similar to Paul's statement in Colossians 3:14: "And over all these virtues put on love, which binds them all together in perfect unity." "Love" is a much broader term than the former, "brotherly kindness," implying self-sacrificial beneficence toward others, whoever they may be (see Luke 10:25-37). Above all, love is defined by the act of God in sending his Son to die (John 3:16).

1:8 For if you possess these qualities in increasing measure, they will keep you from being ineffective and unproductive in your knowledge of our Lord Jesus Christ.

---

[6]See the further discussion of the term in 1:3.

[7]The terms φιλέω (*phileō*) and ἀγαπάω (*agapaō*), as well as their noun forms, are often synonyms, as they are in John 21:15-17.

Peter notes that these qualities are not absolutes, which a Christian either has or does not have. However, the believer will be growing in all these areas and will thereby be effective and productive. Peter makes the point from the negative standpoint, as he warns of "being ineffective and unproductive," probably because that is precisely what had happened to the false teachers about whom he writes in chapter 2. The terms "ineffective" and "unproductive" are near-synonyms in this passage. The first term often refers to workers who are idle, and the second is the common metaphor recalling plants that produce no fruit.

In what way did Peter want his readers to be effective and productive? Although Peter does not specify here, the whole of the letter deals with the holy living that is the fruit of right doctrine. Peter's plea is therefore that his readers will practice these virtues in order to defeat sin, withstand various trials, and serve others. Peter bases these benefits once again in "knowledge of our Lord Jesus Christ." It is fundamentally because believers know Jesus who lived, died, and was resurrected for them that they are able to live holy lives.

1:9 But if anyone does not have them, he is nearsighted and blind, and has forgotten that he has been cleansed from his past sins.

The individual who has not pursued these qualities is unable, or perhaps unwilling, to see the need to put forth the effort to live productively in Christ. That person is "nearsighted and blind," another pair of terms which Peter uses as synonyms for rhetorical effect.[8] This blindness will certainly lead to a life of sinfulness and separation from God. Furthermore, such a person is not only blind but also has amnesia, "having forgotten that he has been cleansed from his past sins." Peter's

---

[8]Technically, nearsightedness is not as bad a condition as blindness. It is possible that the meaning is that the false teachers are "shortsighted," looking to this world and not to the next.

meaning is that Christians are cleansed from sin in order to escape the destruction of sin, not to return to it. Those who sin willfully have therefore failed to live in light of their salvation. So, they are blind to it, or they have forgotten it. The teaching is very much like that of Paul in Romans 6:2: "We died to sin; how can we live in it any longer?" The false teachers troubling Peter's readers were probably like Paul's antagonists, who believed that salvation by grace meant that Christians could deliberately sin without fear of judgment. The language Peter uses here, being "cleansed from past sins," probably refers to the cleansing which takes place at baptism (see Acts 22:16; 1 Cor 6:11 and others).

1:10 Therefore, my brothers, be all the more eager to make your calling and election sure.

Peter concludes and summarizes this section by repeating his exhortation of verse 5, where he encouraged them to "make every effort."[9] The demand is that they live in light of the salvation that has been given to them. Yes, they are among the "called and elect" of God. However, they must not presume upon their salvation by failing to put forth the effort to live holy lives. They must validate that they are God's people (make their "calling and election sure") by living like God's people. A lack of effort to live a holy life is the clearest evidence that a person does not truly belong to God.

Peter's thought is much like that of James, who writes, "Faith itself, if it is not accompanied by action, is dead" (Jas 2:17). Nor is Paul of a different mind, as he writes (even to the Galatians!) that, "I warn you, as I did before, that those who live like this [sexual immorality, impurity, and many others] will not inherit the kingdom of God" (Gal 5:21). John Calvin rightly noted that, "Salvation is by faith alone, but saving faith is never alone."

---

[9]The NIV translation, "be all the more eager," obscures the fact that the same root word (for "effort") is used in both verses.

The terms, "calling" (κλῆσις, *klēsis*) and "election" (ἐκλογή, *eklogē*) are another pair of synonyms, of which Peter is so fond. For more comments on the theology behind these words, see the discussion at verse 3 above, where a form of the term "calling" is also used. Peter believed that salvation is the result of God's initiative, pure grace. However, this in no way relieves humans of responsibility for responding to God's gift. Perhaps the best theological solution to the paradox is the belief that God predetermined to save the world by giving his Son, so that Jesus is ultimately the chosen or "elect" one. By God's grace, he counts among the elect all those who are "in Christ."

For if you do these things, you will never fall,

Peter knows that there is the possibility for Christians to "fall," that is, fail to be welcomed into the eternal kingdom (v. 11). That is what had presumably happened to the false teachers, who were unconcerned with holy living (chapter 2). However, he reassures his readers that their efforts to live in light of their salvation will keep them from falling.[10]

1:11 and you will receive a rich welcome into the eternal kingdom of our Lord and Savior Jesus Christ.

Peter ends the section by focusing on the abundance of God's grace by writing of the "rich welcome" which Christians can expect. "The eternal kingdom" is, of course, the kingdom in its final manifestation, the "new heaven" and "new earth" of 3:13.

Once again, Peter's words are as timely today as the day he penned them. It is easy to fall into the trap of believing that our sins are of no great concern or that we will eventually

---

[10]Peter is in no way teaching that Christians are saved by human effort. First, he does not demand perfect obedience to God's standards. He has made it clear that the Christian life is one of growth, not attainment. Second, even the ability to grow and live holy lives is a gift from God, whose divine power gives everything needed (verse 3). Christians are called simply to work with him rather than against him.

grow out of our sins. In this passage Peter underlines the importance of working hard at spiritual growth. Although the power comes from God, we must make every effort to avail ourselves of it. Failure to do so may result in our failure to "receive a rich welcome into the eternal kingdom."

C. OCCASION: THE APPROACHING DEATH OF PETER (1:12-15)

[12]So I will always remind you of these things, even though you know them and are firmly established in the truth you now have. [13]I think it is right to refresh your memory as long as I live in the tent of this body, [14]because I know that I will soon put it aside, as our Lord Jesus Christ has made clear to me. [15]And I will make every effort to see that after my departure you will always be able to remember these things.

Peter here begins the transition to the main body of his letter. Having begun with an exhortation focusing on his readers (vv. 3-11), he now explains his own circumstances and one of the reasons for writing the letter at this time. In short, he wants to make clear his teaching before he dies.

Many scholars have noted that this letter is very much like a "testament" in this section. The testament or "farewell speech" was a common type of literature among Jews, one in which a hero of the faith would state that he or she was near death. It would usually contain ethical teaching and prophecy about future events which would occur after the hero's death. Since testaments were often fictional, some have suggested that 2 Peter must also be fictional. However, this reasoning is not valid. Not all testaments were fictional, and there is no reason that Peter could not have written one.[11] Furthermore,

---

[11]See Paul's "testament" in Acts 20:17-35.

the fact that 2 Peter contains some elements of a testament does not mean that it ought to be regarded as belonging primarily to this type of literature. Above all, 2 Peter is a letter, like other letters in the New Testament. Writing a letter to loved ones at the end of one's life is hardly an unusual event.

1:12 So I will always remind you of these things, even though you know them and are firmly established in the truth you now have.

The grave importance of living godly lives is what has led Peter to "remind" his readers "of these things," even though they already "know them." These Christians were apparently not novices in the faith, since he describes them as "firmly established in the truth." Peter felt they needed to be reminded again for several reasons: 1) He, one of the great witnesses of the life and teaching of Jesus, is about to die. 2) False teachers have arisen and will continue to disturb the faith of traditional believers. 3) The nature of Christian faith demands the continual retelling of the stories in order for believers to grow.

The surprising thing about this verse is that Peter writes that he "will always remind" them of his teaching. The language here is unusual, and it is not certain that the NIV's "I will always remind you" is the best translation; yet it remains the most likely.[12] So, how is it that a man about to die will continue to communicate to others? Two possibilities seem best: 1) He may think that he will yet live long enough to teach them more. 2) He may intend this letter as a reminder, not only when they receive it but as they read it again and again. Perhaps the second choice is slightly more probable.

1:13 I think it is right to refresh your memory as long as I live in the tent of this body,

Peter repeats his desire to "refresh [their] memory" as he hints for the first time about his approaching death. Peter is

---

[12]See Bauckham, *2 Peter*, p. 195, for the technical grammatical discussion.

simply saying that he is making use of his final days on earth to remind believers of their Christian obligations. To "live in the tent of this body" is a common early Christian way of talking about life in this age, as opposed to life in the coming age. Paul writes similarly in 2 Corinthians 5:1,4: "For we know that if the earthly tent we live in is destroyed, we have a building from God . . . . For while we are in this tent, we groan . . . ." It is important to make clear that Peter is not suggesting that he is awaiting the day when he will become a bodiless spirit after death. It is simply that the physical body is frail, like a tent, and Christians, especially in their later years, look forward to being rid of this "perishable and corruptible" body and receiving a new body at the resurrection. Paul calls the resurrection body a "spiritual body" and teaches that it is imperishable and immortal (1 Cor 15:42-54). While there is much that cannot be known about Christian existence after death, it is important to remember that the Christian view of afterlife involves resurrection of the body, not immortality of the soul as understood in pagan Greek philosophy and religion.[13]

1:14 because I know that I will soon put it aside, as our Lord Jesus Christ has made clear to me.

Peter "knows" that his death is approaching, and that it will come "soon." However, we do not know how soon it was to be. It may have been only days, or it may have been years. Similarly, we do not know just when or how Jesus "made clear" Peter's death to him. He may have received a revelation just prior to his death, or he may be referring here to the event recorded in John 21:18-19: ". . . when you are old you will stretch out your hands, and someone else will dress you and lead you where you do not want to go." It is quite possible that Peter's situation has convinced him that the time referred to by Jesus cannot be far away. Early Christian tradition states

---

[13]See the helpful discussion in Moo, *2 Peter*, pp. 67-68.

that Peter died under the emperor Nero in the mid-60s of the first century. This tradition is probably reliable, unlike the further tradition that states he was crucified upside-down.[14]

The fact that Peter will "put aside" his body does not mean that he does not expect another, better (resurrection) body.[15] While 2 Peter gives few hints regarding the state of the Christian between death and the return of Christ, it makes very clear that believers await "a new heaven and a new earth" (3:13), a situation in which a new body makes perfect sense.

1:15 And I will make every effort to see that after my departure you will always be able to remember these things.

How will Peter ensure that even after his death his readers will be reminded of his teaching? Peter may be suggesting that he "will make every effort" to encourage others to continue to teach what he has taught them.[16] Or he may mean simply that this letter is his effort to help them remember his teaching. In either case, it is clearly important to Peter that his teaching be remembered after his death, as this is his second mention of this concern in this paragraph (see verse 12).

---

[14]In the *Acts of Peter*.

[15]The term translated "put aside" (ἀπόθεσις, *apothesis*) is the term for taking off clothes, so that the NIV has obscured Peter's (admittedly mixed) metaphor.

[16]Moo, *2 Peter*, p. 63, notes that the Gospel of Mark is, according to tradition, the memoirs of Peter. Mark was present with Peter at the end of Peter's life according to 1 Peter 5:13.

II. BODY OF LETTER (1:16–3:13)

A. REASONS FOR BELIEVING IN CHRIST'S RETURN (1:16-21)

1. Peter's Eyewitness Testimony (1:16-18)

[16]We did not follow cleverly invented stories when we told you about the power and coming of our Lord Jesus Christ, but we were eyewitnesses of his majesty. [17]For he received honor and glory from God the Father when the voice came to him from the Majestic Glory, saying, "This is my Son, whom I love; with him I am well pleased."[a] [18]We ourselves heard this voice that came from heaven when we were with him on the sacred mountain.

[a]17 Matt. 17:5; Mark 9:7; Luke 9:35

Peter now begins the body of the letter, as he introduces the main topic that will occupy him throughout the remainder of the letter. His great concern is the Second Coming of Jesus. He will first offer reasons to believe, and then he will attack those who are denying Christ's return. Finally, he will remind his readers of the truth about the event, followed by concluding exhortations to faithfulness.

This small section (verses 16-18) and the next (19-21) offer Peter's readers evidence to support his teaching about the Second Coming. The first evidence is that Peter and those with him were eyewitnesses to a miracle which looked ahead to and therefore guaranteed the return of Jesus in glory.

1:16 We did not follow cleverly invented stories when we told you about the power and coming of our Lord Jesus Christ, but we were eyewitnesses of his majesty.
Why did Peter feel the need to tell his readers that it was not on the basis of "cleverly invented stories" that his teaching about the return of Jesus rested? It is very probable that

those who denied the Second Coming were claiming that Jesus had never promised a return. The very idea of Jesus coming back, they would say, was a creation of some very imaginative and clever people. While we know less than we might wish to know about these false teachers, we do know that even in the first century there were a number who claimed to be Christian who flatly denied the doctrine of resurrection (and, by implication, Jesus' future return).[17]

It is somewhat difficult for those who are the beneficiaries of centuries of orthodox teaching on this matter to understand how anyone could take such a stand. However, there are several things modern Christians should keep in mind. First, the early Christians had no New Testament on which to rely. They had to rely on what they heard from church leaders. It was difficult for them to distinguish what was true from what was false. Second, many came out of a pagan Greek thought-world in which life after death was ridiculed. Most Greeks believed in a very impersonal immortality of the soul if they believed in afterlife at all. They may have reasoned that Jesus could not have been resurrected and therefore could certainly not come again. Paul had to deal with such thinking on many occasions, including that behind 2 Timothy 2:18, where two men had apparently "spiritualized" the resurrection: "They say that the resurrection has already taken place, and they destroy the faith of some." Third, many of the earliest Christians expected Jesus to return during their lifetimes. When he failed to do so, they became disillusioned and therefore became more susceptible to the Greek thinking about the future. Fourth, then just as now, immoral living helps to create false teaching. Those who did not want to give up their sinful lifestyles had to discover ways of justifying or at least living with their sin. One way to do so was (and is) to deny those teachings of Christianity which would restrict their desired activities.

---

[17]See 1 Corinthians 15:12; 2 Timothy 2:18.

Peter has changed from using the singular ("I") to the plural ("we") in order to remind his readers that others (according to the Gospels, James and John) were also "eyewitnesses" to the Transfiguration. It is obvious that Peter is referring to the Transfiguration as he writes of the certainty of the "power and coming" of Jesus. This pair of terms should be understood as one idea, the "powerful coming" or "coming in power." It is also clear that Peter is writing about the Second Coming. However, it is not as clear why Peter thinks that the Transfiguration is evidence for the future Second Coming of Christ.

The answer lies in the proper understanding of the Transfiguration. It was not a miracle simply designed to impress the apostles and show that Jesus was indeed sent from God. The various elements of the Gospel account of the story must be examined in order to understand Peter's reasoning. The Transfiguration occurs in the Gospels (Matt 17; Mark 9; Luke 9) immediately after Peter's revelation that Jesus is the Messiah. Jesus follows Peter's confession with his own revelation that the Son of Man was to come in judgment "when he comes in the glory of his Father with the holy angels" (Mark 8:38, NRSV). It is in this context that Jesus is glorified above even Moses and Elijah, when God tells those who are present to "listen to him." As we will see below, the allusion made by the voice of God makes it plain that Jesus is the one who will subdue the nations and reign as God's appointed judge and ruler. The Transfiguration then was a preview for Peter and those with him of Jesus' final glory and power, which would be inaugurated with the Second Coming.

1:17 For he received honor and glory from God the Father when the voice came to him from the Majestic Glory, saying, "This is my Son, whom I love; with him I am well pleased."

Peter uses yet another pair of words, "honor and glory," to describe what Jesus received on the mountain. Whether the honor is associated with the voice and the glory with the shining face and clothes or whether both terms describe the whole event makes little difference. What matters is that Peter understands that the event was God's appointment (or at least acknowledgement) of Jesus as final judge and king.

Peter does not quite state that the voice on the mountain came directly from God, tracing its origin rather to the "Majestic Glory."[18] The use of the term "Majestic Glory" is due to the common Jewish practice of avoiding the use of the name of God, in keeping with the third commandment. The words spoken by the voice are a further indicator of the significance of the event. The words are a partial quotation of Psalm 2:7 ("This is my Son") and Isaiah 42:1 ("with whom I am well pleased"). Psalm 2 envisions God laughing at those who oppose his appointed king and warning of the coming destruction of his enemies. That Peter understood this background is clear from his use in verse 18 of the phrase "the sacred mountain" from Psalm 2:6. The quotation of Isaiah 42:1 equates Jesus with the suffering servant of God.

1:18 We ourselves heard this voice that came from heaven when we were with him on the sacred mountain.

Peter reiterates the fact that he and his companions were eyewitnesses (or ear-witnesses) as he ends this short section. His intent is that his readers be impressed that his teaching about the return of Christ came directly from God himself. They might also be impressed that the one writing the letter to them was one of those chosen to be with Jesus on that occasion. The term "sacred mountain," as noted above, indicates that Peter knew and relied upon the larger context of Psalm 2 for his understanding of the Transfiguration.

2. The Sure Prophetic Word (1:19-21)

[19]**And we have the word of the prophets made more certain, and you will do well to pay attention to it, as to a light**

---

[18]For parallels and further discussion, see Bauckham, *2 Peter*, p. 218.

shining in a dark place, until the day dawns and the morning star rises in your hearts. **²⁰Above all, you must understand that no prophecy of Scripture came about by the
prophet's own interpretation. ²¹For prophecy never had its
origin in the will of man, but men spoke from God as they
were carried along by the Holy Spirit.**

Peter's second piece of evidence in support of his teaching
about Christ's return is the teaching of Scripture. Peter's con-
tention is that the prophets prophesied that Christ would
return. The Second Coming is not predicated upon cleverly
invented stories. This section also functions as a transition to
the next section, since it deals with the words of the biblical
prophets. Chapter 2 will discuss another group of prophets,
the false prophets of Peter's day.

**1:19 And we have the word of the prophets made more cer-
tain,**

Every teaching or prediction of the prophets is for Peter
and for his readers a "certain" word already. After all, their
Bible is the Old Testament, including the writings of prophets.
The statement here, however, suggests that it is made even
"more certain" by the Transfiguration event. Just in case
there were any doubts about the teachings of the prophets
concerning God's plans for world history, Peter's (and the
other apostles') eyewitness testimony should rule them out.
The assumption here is that the Old Testament prophets
spoke of the future Second Coming of God's Messiah, an
assumption shared by all New Testament writers.

**and you will do well to pay attention to it, as to a light shin-
ing in a dark place, until the day dawns and the morning
star rises in your hearts.**

Peter directs his readers' attention to the words of the
prophets by comparing prophecy to "a light shining in a dark
place." The metaphor is a common one in Jewish literature,

the best known in Psalm 119:105: "Your word is a lamp to my feet and a light for my path." However, Peter extends the metaphor, suggesting that the light of prophecy will be needed during the night that lasts "until the day dawns and the morning star rises in your hearts." In the context of 2 Peter that "day" can only be the return of Christ, especially in light of the reference to the "morning star." The allusion is to a messianic text, Numbers 24:17: "A star will come out of Jacob."[19]

It is somewhat surprising that the metaphor includes the rising of the star in the "hearts" of Peter's readers. Yet the whole context refers to the return of Jesus, a time of great joy which was eagerly anticipated in the hearts of the early Christians. Paul's words may help the modern reader feel the excitement: "For the Lord himself will come down from heaven, with a loud command, with the voice of the archangel and with the trumpet call of God, and the dead in Christ will rise first. After that, we who are still alive and are left will be caught up together with them in the clouds to meet the Lord in the air. And so we will be with the Lord forever" (1 Thess 4:16-17). It appears that Peter, like Paul, envisions the possibility that the Lord will return during the lifetime of his readers, since he speaks not of their deaths but of the day dawning on them.

1:20 Above all, you must understand that no prophecy of Scripture came about by the prophet's own interpretation.

The NIV translation is quite interpretive here, since the original is somewhat ambiguous.[20] The major part of the sentence may also be translated, "No prophecy of Scripture is a matter of one's own interpretation" (NRSV). This translation would imply that Peter is objecting to the private (and

---

[19]See Revelation 22:16 for a similar usage of this text.

[20]The ambiguity arises because of a Greek word (ἐπίλυσις, *epilysis*) with several possible meanings, a pronoun (ἴδιος, *idios*, "one's own") without a clear antecedent, and a Greek verb (γίνεται, *ginetai*) with an unclear function. See Bauckham, *2 Peter*, pp. 229-233, for the full discussion of this very technical matter.

incorrect) interpretation of prophecy practiced by the false teachers. However, this understanding does not suit well the preceding (19) and especially the following verse (21). The NIV interpretation seems best.

The false teachers have rejected not only the teaching of Peter and the other apostles about the coming of Christ but also the teachings of the prophets about this event. Their judgment may have been that God never inspired such prophecies but that the prophets were wrongly interpreting their visions or whatever signs God may have given them. Therefore Peter asserts that all prophecy in Scripture originated with God, not with the prophet. That is to say that not only the visions or dreams came from God but so did the prophets' understanding of them. This seems to be the point of the next verse.

1:21 For prophecy never had its origin in the will of man, but men spoke from God as they were carried along by the Holy Spirit.

If the false teachers contended that the prophets gave their own (wrong) interpretation of God's visions, then Peter has responded in verse 20 that the prophets did not voice their own understandings. He now needs only to state what the origin of prophecy was. It originated not "in the will of man" but was rather "from God," through the agency of "the Holy Spirit."

2 PETER 2

B. WARNING AGAINST FALSE TEACHERS (2:1-22)

1. The Coming of False Teachers (2:1-3)

¹But there were also false prophets among the people, just as there will be false teachers among you. They will secretly introduce destructive heresies, even denying the sovereign Lord who bought them — bringing swift destruction on themselves. ²Many will follow their shameful ways and will bring the way of truth into disrepute. ³In their greed these teachers will exploit you with stories they have made up. Their condemnation has long been hanging over them, and their destruction has not been sleeping.

With this section Peter gets to the heart of his reason for writing the letter. False teachers are about, and their teachings are not only wrong but absolutely destructive to Christian living. They will be severely punished, but they will first do terrible harm to God's people. Peter wants to ensure that his readers are not among those who will be led astray.

One of the great questions for the interpretation of this chapter concerns the time referent. Peter speaks of what the false teachers *will* do (future tense) in verses 1-3, yet in the remainder of the chapter speaks of what they are doing (present) or have done (past). A number of explanations have been offered. 1) A standard explanation of many critical scholars is that the letter was actually written long after the death of Peter, when the false teachers were active. The writer attributed these words to Peter as a prophetic warning for a later generation. The writer chose Peter either because his teachings were consistent with those of Peter or because he simply wanted to use a name which carried authority. The different tenses, then, are the result of the writer not carrying through with his fiction about Peter writing well before the events. The writer slipped up, so to speak, and revealed himself to be from a later generation. 2) The future tense is used in the early verses because Peter expects the situation to get worse. That is, false teachers were present, but more were to come. 3) The use of the future tense was simply a rhetorical device, and no time reference was intended. 4) The false teachers are not yet with Peter's readers, but he anticipates that they soon will be. He therefore speaks of their future arrival, but he knows of their present and past teachings and lifestyles. 5) In verses 1-3 Peter is quoting the substance of prophetic warnings from Jesus and early Christian prophets. For example, in the Olivet Discourse Jesus speaks of coming false teachers (Matt 24:11,24). Peter's "quotation" of earlier warnings therefore includes their use of the future tense. Peter thereby implies that even Jesus warned of these heretics, giving his readers even greater courage to reject the false teaching.

It is argued in the introduction to the commentary that there is no overwhelming reason to deny the Petrine authorship of 2 Peter. Therefore the first solution above should be rejected. It is difficult to know which of the other explanations may be correct, although I favor option 2 or 4. Fortunately, having the right answer to this question is not essential for understanding this section of the letter.

A further matter already discussed in the introduction is the question of this letter's relation to Jude. The great similarities to Jude begin in these verses, and it is probable that the two are somehow related literarily. However, we cannot be certain whether Jude used Peter's work or vice versa. Our understanding of these verses will therefore not be based on any theory of dependence.

2:1 But there were also false prophets among the people, just as there will be false teachers among you.

Peter's discussion of prophets who "spoke from God" in the previous verses provides the transition to the present warning that "there will be false teachers among you."[1] Here Peter turns the tables on the false teachers, by arguing that it was not the biblical prophets who spoke falsely about the Second Coming — it is rather the false teachers who are playing the role of the Old Testament "false prophets." It is interesting that Peter uses the term "false teachers" for his opponents rather than "false prophets." Most likely these men did not claim to be prophets.

They will secretly introduce destructive heresies, even denying the sovereign Lord who bought them — bringing swift destruction on themselves.

Peter attacks in the strongest of terms, exposing these men on several fronts. First, they do their work "secretly." This probably suggests that they have pretended to be what they are not, in order to gain a hearing. Second, their teachings are "destructive." Since the term translated "heresies" was not yet a synonym for "unorthodox teaching," the emphasis here is probably on the destructive nature of their opinions.[2] Peter will shortly give abundant evidence for his teaching that false thinking leads to sinful behavior that eventually leads to destruction. Third, the false teachers go so far as to "deny the

---

[1] See the discussion immediately above on the use of the future tense in these verses.

[2] The term "heresy" (αἵρεσις, *hairesis*) is used elsewhere in the New Testament simply to refer to different philosophical schools or religious sects (Acts 5:17; 15:5; 24:5) or to factions in the early church (Gal 5:20). See the discussion in Bauckham, *2 Peter*, p. 239.

sovereign Lord."[3] Only here is it implied that they deny
Christ, and one might think that the denial of Christ (as
Messiah or as Son of God) would be the central concern of
Peter in this letter. For that reason, most think that they were
denying Christ by denying his future return or by denying his
lordship in practice (by immoral behavior). Either or both of
these may be in Peter's thoughts.

The mention of "the sovereign Lord who bought them"
reminds Peter's readers that Christ has an absolute claim on
Christians as their new master. The (common) metaphor pic-
tures Christians as slaves, purchased by a "sovereign Lord,"
the NIV's translation of the unusual term δεσπότης (*despotēs*),
from which arose the English word "despot." The purchase
price in Peter's mind was without doubt the cross. Peter's
point is that these false teachers by their teaching and actions
were in fact denying the very one who died in order to free
them from their former masters, sin and death. This can only
bring "swift destruction" on them. God will not long tolerate
this deliberate rebellion.

**2:2 Many will follow their shameful ways and will bring the
way of truth into disrepute.**

Unfortunately, false teachers usually gain a following. The
reason is that the false teaching always has an attractive element to it, in this case its "shameful ways." The term normally
indicates sensual immorality, most often of a sexual nature.
Peter will be much more specific about these sins later in this
chapter, where he writes of their sexual excesses and greed.

Tragically, their sins will harm not only themselves but also
"the way of truth." This phrase is roughly equivalent to "the
Christian way of life," pointing to the ethical conduct of
Christians.[4] The verb translated "bring . . . into disrepute"

---

[3]Very similar language is used in Jude 4.

[4]It was common in Jewish literature to use the term "way" to describe
the ethical behavior of God's people. The writer of Acts uses the term

(βλασφημέω, *blasphēmeō*) shows that Peter is alluding to the Greek translation of Isaiah 52:5: "Because of you my name is continually blasphemed among the Gentiles." Peter's concern here is that non-Christians will speak badly of the Christian way of life, severely hindering the church from carrying out its mission.

2:3 In their greed these teachers will exploit you with stories they have made up.

This is the first of several times Peter accuses his opponents of greed. How is it that they were profiting from their activity? They were almost certainly being supported by the churches in which they taught. After all, Jesus said, "The worker deserves his wages" (Luke 10:7), and Paul further argued the point in 1 Corinthians 9.

There are few hints to help the modern interpreter know what sort of "stories" the false teachers may have told. However, contending that they have "made up" the stories is Peter's way of using his opponents' arguments against them. They accused the apostles of following "cleverly invented stories," according to 1:16. So Peter here writes that they are the ones who are making things up.

Their condemnation has long been hanging over them, and their destruction has not been sleeping.

Peter states that the condemnation of these false teachers was pronounced long ago.[5] Perhaps he means that the Old Testament pronouncements against false prophets apply to these men. More likely, though, he is thinking that the destruction that came upon people like them in the Old Testament is clear enough evidence that the same will come upon these false teachers. The next seven verses, rehearsing the destruction of

---

as a designation for the early church ("the Way" in Acts 9:2; 19:9; and others).

[5]There is a close parallel in Jude 4.

many ungodly groups, are the explanation of this sentence, as the beginning "for" in verse 4 indicates.

Most interestingly, Peter apparently is using the false teachers' words against them. They probably were ridiculing the idea of the Second Coming by statements such as, "God's judgment is idle, and his punishment is asleep." Peter's quotation of their taunt in 3:4 and his response in 3:9 further suggest the possibility of such statements. If they indeed uttered such words, Peter's choice of words is very deliberate: "Their condemnation . . . has not been idle, and their destruction is not asleep" (NRSV).

Readers should pay close attention to the nature of the false teaching here in 2 Peter and throughout the New Testament. Those who are labeled "false teachers" are typically those who are denying a central doctrine of Christianity. For example, some denied that Jesus came in the flesh (1 John 4:2); others taught that the resurrection of believers had already taken place (1 Timothy 2:18). Many others taught that sins of the flesh were of no concern. When central Christian teachings are being denied, Christians must do as Peter, Paul, and John did. We must stamp out the error. However, some have taken texts about false teachers out of context and applied them to everyone who holds a different opinion from theirs. Modern Christians should take their cue from the apostles and attack only those who uphold the sort of teachings of the false teachers in the New Testament.

2. The Condemnation of False Teachers (2:4-10a)

⁴For if God did not spare angels when they sinned, but sent them to hell,ᵃ putting them into gloomy dungeonsᵇ to be held for judgment; ⁵if he did not spare the ancient world when he brought the flood on its ungodly people, but protected Noah, a preacher of righteousness, and seven others; ⁶if he condemned the cities of Sodom and Gomorrah by

burning them to ashes, and made them an example of what is going to happen to the ungodly; [7]and if he rescued Lot, a righteous man, who was distressed by the filthy lives of lawless men [8](for that righteous man, living among them day after day, was tormented in his righteous soul by the lawless deeds he saw and heard) — [9]if this is so, then the Lord knows how to rescue godly men from trials and to hold the unrighteous for the day of judgment, while continuing their punishment.[c] [10]This is especially true of those who follow the corrupt desire of the sinful nature[d] and despise authority.

[a]4 Greek *Tartarus*   [b]4 Some manuscripts *into chains of darkness*   [c]9 Or *unrighteous for punishment until the day of judgment*   [d]10 Or *the flesh*

Verses 4-9 comprise one of the longest sentences in the NIV Bible. The translators were unable to follow their usual practice of breaking long sentences into smaller ones, because verses 4-8 provide a protasis (the "if" statement) and verse 9 (and verse 10 in the original) give the apodosis (the "then" statement). The point could hardly be clearer: God has always brought certain destruction upon those who rebelliously follow their sinful desires, and at the same time he has protected those who remain faithful to him. If he did so then, he can be counted on to do the same with regard to these Christians and the false teachers who are afflicting them (see v. 3b).

Peter reminds these believers of three stories of God's judgment upon rebellious sinfulness, two of which include God's protection of godly people in the midst of the those who were destroyed. There are obvious parallels with Jude 5-7.

2:4 For if God did not spare angels when they sinned, but sent them to hell, putting them into gloomy dungeons to be held for judgment;

The next two examples of God's judgment (the flood, Sodom and Gomorrah) are much easier to understand than this one concerning sinning angels. There is no absolutely clear Old Testament text which describes such an event. The mysterious allusions to fallen angels in Ezekiel 28:11-19 and Isaiah 14:12-17 are possibly in Peter's mind, but there is no reference to gloomy dungeons in hell in those texts. It is far more likely, as many scholars have suggested, that Peter has in mind Genesis 6:1-4 and the Jewish traditions about these verses.[6] The Genesis story is about the sons of God (a frequent designation for angels) who married and had children with "the daughters of men." The intertestamental writing 1 Enoch tells the story of God punishing these angels by confining them to the darkness of the underworld (see 1 Enoch 10:4-6).[7] The story therefore fits very well Peter's allusion.

Several observations further suggest that Peter has in mind this story. First, the parallel passage in Jude alludes to the same story (verse 6), and Jude explicitly quotes 1 Enoch in verses 14-15.[8] Second, Peter apparently makes reference to these confined angels ("spirits in prison") in 1 Peter 3:19 (see comments there). Third, Peter's three examples of God's judgment are probably intended to be in chronological order (Gen 6:1-4; 6:5-8:22; 19:1-29).[9]

The word translated "cast . . . into hell" in the NIV is actually a word from Greek mythology meaning "cast into Tartarus." Tartarus was the underworld into which rebellious spirits and humans were sent. Peter makes it clear that this is a (horrible) holding place for them until the day of judgment. It is thus not quite the same as hell. The phrase, "gloomy dungeons," is an accurate description of the place of punishment described in 1 Enoch.

---

[6]1 Enoch 6-9, 86-88, and others; Jubilees 4:15,22; 5:1; CD 2:17-19; T. Reub. 5:6-7, and several others.

[7]This tradition was quite well known in the first century, as other Jewish writings also make reference to the story. See Bauckham, *2 Peter*, p. 51.

[8]Many Christians have wondered how Peter (and Jude) could refer to such a story told in (pseudonymous) 1 Enoch. It is probably best to understand this story to be simply a well-known story that would provide a good illustration for Peter.

[9]Moo, *2 Peter*, p. 102.

2:5 if he did not spare the ancient world when he brought the flood on its ungodly people, but protected Noah, a preacher of righteousness, and seven others;

Peter's second example of God's judgment is closely related to the first. In Genesis 6:5 and in the story in 1 Enoch the sinful "sons of God" are partly responsible for the growing sinfulness of humanity which leads to the flood. In Peter's former story, the angels are punished. In this story, the people are punished.

It is not surprising that Peter uses the flood story to remind his readers that "the ancient world" was destroyed because the people were "ungodly." Nor is it surprising that he mentions Noah and those with him being "protected." After all, his goal is to give confidence to his godly readers while warning them about the ungodly false teachers. It may be surprising, though, that he calls Noah "a preacher of righteousness." The Genesis story never mentions Noah's preaching, although a number of nonbiblical Jewish works fill in that void.[10] Peter may be referring to these traditions, or he may be referring to the unspoken "preaching" of building an ark for 120 years.

The mention of "seven others" obscures the original, "the eighth Noah," an idiom which means, "Noah and seven others." The reference to eight in the original reminds the attentive reader of 1 Peter 3:20, which also mentions the eight who were saved, immediately after the mention of the "spirits in prison" (see verse 4). More importantly, the number reminds the believers that the godly are often found in small numbers.

2:6 if he condemned the cities of Sodom and Gomorrah by burning them to ashes, and made them an example of what is going to happen to the ungodly;

Peter's third story of punishment for the ungodly and protection for the righteous is the story of Sodom and Gomorrah

---

[10]Bauckham, *2 Peter*, pp. 250-251.

and of Lot.[11] It may be worth noting that this story, like the earlier two, seems to revolve around punishment for sexual sin. The angels in verse 4 lust and have illicit sexual relations with women, leading to their punishment. The offspring of this sexual union lead the world even further into rebellion, and all but eight people are destroyed. Similarly, in Genesis 19 it is the men following their basest sexual desires that leads to the destruction of Sodom and Gomorrah. (Peter refers to the "filthy lives of lawless men" in the next verse.) In verses 13-14 Peter will accuse his opponents of the same. Here he assures his readers that their fate will also be like that of Sodom and Gomorrah.

2:7 and if he rescued Lot, a righteous man, who was distressed by the filthy lives of lawless men 2:8 (for that righteous man, living among them day after day, was tormented in his righteous soul by the lawless deeds he saw and heard) —

Peter's readers can be assured that God will take care of them as he took care of Lot (and Noah). Even in the midst of people destined for utter destruction, God's people will be "rescued."

Modern readers are somewhat surprised that the adjective "righteous" is used to describe Lot. The Genesis narratives show him to be wavering and cowardly (although some later Jewish writings improved upon his moral stature).[12] However, Lot does emerge from the stories a righteous, though tragic, character. The Genesis narrative shows him to be one who believed and trusted God, despite some obvious failings. He protected his visitors from the men of Sodom and pleaded with the Sodomites not to do "this wicked thing." For Peter, Lot's being "distressed" about their "filthy lives" is what shows his righteousness, since he mentions again that Lot was "tormented in his righteous

---

[11]Jesus also calls his listeners to faithfulness by referring to the stories of the flood and of Sodom (Luke 17:26-32).

[12]See Bauckham, *2 Peter*, p. 252.

soul." Peter assumes that this occurred "day after day," since Lot was "living among them." Perhaps one can be considered "righteous" if, even though weak, he is distressed and tormented by the evil around and within him.

2:9 if this is so, then the Lord knows how to rescue godly men from trials and to hold the unrighteous for the day of judgment, while continuing their punishment.

After four "if" statements, Peter finally provides the "then." If God has been faithful in the past, then he will be so in the future. The "godly men," Noah and Lot, were rescued from God's worst destruction against the ungodly. This must have been comforting to Peter's readers, who were being told that there would be no final judgment for the immoral and thus no salvation or protection for those who are distressed and tormented by immorality.

The Greek term translated "while continuing their punishment" may also be understood to mean that the ungodly are going "to be punished" at the day of judgment (rather than while waiting). However, the NIV has chosen the more natural grammatical understanding and that which is supported by verse 4. "The unrighteous" who are being punished while awaiting "the day of judgment" include at least the fallen angels who were consigned to the gloomy dungeons. But does Peter imply here that all the unrighteous dead are experiencing punishment while they await judgment? This is probably his intention since this was the common early Christian opinion and since this statement would appear to refer to more than simply the fallen angels.

2:10 This is especially true of those who follow the corrupt desire of the sinful nature and despise authority.

Peter does not have to refer specifically to the false teachers for all readers to know he has them in mind. The two broad categories of sin of which they are guilty are 1) "indulging their flesh in depraved lust" (NRSV, a better translation here than

that of the NIV), and 2) "despising authority." The terms used
in the first charge suggest that in their sexual sins they have
made a god of "the flesh" (σάρξ, *sarx*). The term means not
"the physical body" but, as the NIV well translates, "the sinful
nature" or the sinful tendency within human beings.

The false teachers' contempt for authority has been hinted
at already. They apparently have spoken against the apostles
(1:16) and the prophets (1:20). They also "slander celestial
beings," as the next sentence states (2:10b). Most seriously,
they also deny "the sovereign Lord" (2:1). Peter's statement
here probably refers to all of these (and more). These men
are unwilling to answer to any but themselves and their lusts.
However, willing or not, they will answer to the God who has
always punished willful sinfulness.

3. The Sins of the False Teachers (2:10b-16)

**Bold and arrogant, these men are not afraid to slan-
der celestial beings; ¹¹yet even angels, although they are
stronger and more powerful, do not bring slanderous accusations against such beings in the presence of the Lord.
¹²But these men blaspheme in matters they do not under-
stand. They are like brute beasts, creatures of instinct, born
only to be caught and destroyed, and like beasts they too
will perish.**

**¹³They will be paid back with harm for the harm they have
done. Their idea of pleasure is to carouse in broad daylight.
They are blots and blemishes, reveling in their pleasures
while they feast with you.^a ¹⁴With eyes full of adultery, they
never stop sinning; they seduce the unstable; they are experts
in greed — an accursed brood! ¹⁵They have left the straight
way and wandered off to follow the way of Balaam son of
Beor, who loved the wages of wickedness. ¹⁶But he was
rebuked for his wrongdoing by a donkey — a beast without**

speech — who spoke with a man's voice and restrained the prophet's madness.

ᵃ13 Some manuscripts *in their love feasts*

Peter has already written of the coming of the false teachers and their future condemnation. He has also offered Old Testament examples of the sort of destruction that awaits them. In this section he gives his most detailed description of their attitude and behavior. They are ignorant, arrogant, adulterous, and greedy.

Bold and arrogant, these men are not afraid to slander celestial beings;

"These men," the false teachers, not only despise authority, but they are "bold and arrogant" about it. Since they do not believe in a final judgment, they are afraid of nothing and no one. Already we learned that they did not accept the words of the apostles (1:16) or that of the prophets (1:20). Peter now writes that they "slander celestial beings." The NIV rendering is again interpretive, understanding the term "glorious ones" (δόξας, *doxas*) as "celestial beings," without naming them as good (angels) or evil (demons). Although a few have argued that human authority figures should be included in this term, there are good reasons for the NIV interpretation. First, in the parallel text, Jude 8, the term clearly refers to angelic beings. (Note that Jude goes on to mention the story of the archangel Michael disputing with the devil, but not slandering him.) Second, the next verse in 2 Peter makes most sense if these beings are spiritual beings rather than human beings (see below).

But just who are these celestial beings the false teachers are slandering? And why are they slandering them? Peter gives few hints. We will never know for sure, but we can make some educated guesses. Perhaps the slandered spiritual beings are demonic forces, whose very existence the false teachers deny. Perhaps the false teachers have not accepted teachings such as those of Paul, who writes, "For our struggle is not against flesh and blood, but against the rulers, against the authorities, against the powers of this dark world and against the spiritual forces of evil in the heavenly realms" (Eph 6:12). It is not difficult to imagine that they ridiculed those who would warn them that their sinful behavior puts them in great danger of coming under the control of these forces.

2:11 yet even angels, although they are stronger and more powerful, do not bring slanderous accusations against such beings in the presence of the Lord.

The celestial beings of verse 10 must be evil spiritual beings, since "even" angels refrain from accusing them. But why does Peter note that angels do not slander "such beings?" And to what story is he alluding? The parallel in Jude may shed light in this case, since it provides an example of an angel who refrained from accusing an evil spiritual being. Jude 9 refers to an intertestamental Jewish writing called the *Assumption of Moses*, in which the archangel Michael argues with the devil over the body of Moses. Even though the devil has slandered Moses by accusing him of murder, Michael leaves the accusation of the devil up to God, saying, "The Lord rebuke you!"[13]

Angels are "stronger and more powerful" than human beings, as evidenced by many biblical stories. Perhaps the first in the mind of Peter's readers would be the angels who came to Abraham to tell him of the future destruction of Sodom and Gomorrah. These angels struck blind the men of Sodom, and they later called down burning sulfur on the cities.

---

[13]Of course, we are not certain that Peter is thinking about this story. If he is familiar with the letter of Jude, he is intentionally omitting direct reference to this story. If he does not know Jude, there is no reason at all to surmise that he has this story in mind. It seems slightly more probable that Peter knows the story but omits the reference to it for some reason. Perhaps his readers would not be familiar with it.

The point is that even with their God-given power, angels do not take lightly the power of evil spiritual beings. The devil and his forces are not to be underestimated. They have destroyed many foolish victims.

Much has been said and written in recent years about "spiritual warfare," guardian angels, demonic forces and the like. Much of this has been speculation, and some has been clearly unbiblical. A lot of bad advice has been given about how to do battle against the demonic powers. However, it is also dangerous to underestimate the power of spiritual forces, as this text suggests.

2:12 But these men blaspheme in matters they do not understand.

It is always poor judgment to speak against that which one does not understand. It is especially foolish to revile those with superior power and a desire to destroy. The fact that these teachers are ignorant about these forces is no excuse, because they are ignorant by their own choice. It is a common theme throughout Scripture that those who have chosen to ignore the truth are just as guilty as those who know it and disobey.

They are like brute beasts, creatures of instinct, born only to be caught and destroyed, and like beasts they too will perish. 2:13 They will be paid back with harm for the harm they have done.

Peter draws an important distinction between humans and mere animals, categorizing these foolish men with the "brute [ἄλογα, *aloga*, "unreasoning"] beasts" that were "born only" to be slaughtered for their meat. Rather than following reason and revelation, the false teachers are guided only by their ignorance and sinful desires. Their arrogance and their passion for wealth and sexual indulgence (vv. 13-16) will ensure that "they too will perish."[14] Peter then employs a pun to state

---

[14]The last phrase in the NIV is an interpretation of an ambiguous origi-

that the coming destruction of the false teachers will be God's retribution: they will receive harm for inflicting harm.[15]

Their idea of pleasure is to carouse in broad daylight.

This sentence begins Peter's clearest description of their sins, the first of which is that they "carouse." The term τρυφή (*tryphē*) implies self-indulgence, the gratification of the basic appetites without restraint. The false teachers are shown to be bold and arrogant even in their carousing, since they practice it "in broad daylight." Sexual sin, drunkenness, and other sensual excesses were generally practiced at night in the first century, just as now.

They are blots and blemishes, reveling in their pleasures while they feast with you.

The interpretation of this sentence may be helped by noting its parallel in Jude 12. There Jude speaks of the false teachers as "blemishes at your love feasts" (Jude 12). The term "love feasts" (ἀγάπαις, *agapais*) there refers to the fellowship meals during which the Lord's supper was eaten. This may explain Peter's reference to the "feasting" in this verse.

---

nal text. The original reads literally, "in their destruction (or corruption) they also will be destroyed" (see Bauckham, *2 Peter*, p. 263). If "corruption" should be read instead of "destruction," Peter means that their moral corruption will destroy them. But "destruction" is probably better, since the same term is used earlier in the verse to describe the killing of the animals. The antecedent of the term "their" is a more difficult problem. It may refer to the evil angels (celestial beings), meaning "when the evil angels are destroyed, the false teachers will also be destroyed." Or it may refer to the animals, suggesting the reading, "when the animals are destroyed, the false teachers will be destroyed," or the NIV's meaning, "the false teachers will be destroyed like the animals." Fortunately, we need not have a final solution to this problem to understand the primary point: the false teachers will surely perish for their deeds.

[15]The English only partially reflects the word-play, using the word harm twice. Different but similar-sounding words are used in Greek (ἀδικούμενοι [*adikoumenoi*], ἀδικίας [*adikias*]).

The term *agapais* (love feasts) may also have suggested Peter's term for pleasures, ἀπάταις (*apatais*).

Peter's terms, "blots and blemishes," are another pair of synonyms. The terms look ahead to 3:14, where Christians are encouraged to be found "*without* spot or blemish" at the Second Coming. The terms therefore also look back to the Jewish sacrificial system: the sacrificial animals were to be without blemish. Peter's point, then, is that these men are sinful and unacceptable blemishes on what is otherwise a holy gathering of Christians.

The false teachers not only follow their sinful desires ("reveling in their pleasures"), but they do so when the church is gathered to "feast" together. As in Jude 12, the reference is probably to the regular shared meals of the church. Perhaps we are to understand that the false teachers were guilty of gluttony and drunkenness at the very time they were supposed to have been celebrating their redemption from sin in the cross of Jesus.

2:14 With eyes full of adultery, they never stop sinning; they seduce the unstable;

The phrase, "eyes full of adultery," means literally that they are always looking for an adulteress. The next words, "they never stop sinning," also refers to the eyes of these men. They are constantly seeking someone with whom they can commit adultery. Unfortunately, they are sometimes successful, because there are among the Christians some who are not well grounded. These "unstable" Christians are without doubt the target of much of the "teaching" of these false teachers. Peter accuses them in verse 18 of preying upon new converts.

they are experts in greed — an accursed brood!

As mentioned in 2:3, Peter's antagonists are greedy. The term in Greek is much like the term in English. A person can be greedy for money, sex, power, and more. But it probably refs primarily to financial gain, since the next verse recalls a greedy Old Testament false prophet. The false teachers have found a way to profit financially from their activities, probably being supported by the church for their teaching. The NIV attempts with the word "expert" to translate a vivid phrase, "having hearts *well trained* [γεγυμνασμένην, *gegymnasmenēn*] in greed." Not only are they greedy — they have worked at it and perfected it.

Writing that they are "an accursed brood" is Peter's way of reminding his readers again that these men are doomed to destruction. No matter how impressive and successful they appear to be, they stand under God's curse.

2:15 They have left the straight way and wandered off to follow the way of Balaam son of Beor, who loved the wages of wickedness.

Peter has already mentioned "the way of truth" in 2:2. Now he writes of "the straight way," a common metaphor in Jewish and early Christian literature. The straight way is the way of holy living, but these men have "wandered off" the path, just as Balaam the son of Beor did. The NIV translation ignores the fact that the best Greek manuscripts read "son of Bosor" rather than "son of Beor." Balaam is nowhere else called by this name, but the term may be an intentional mixing of the term "Beor" with the term for "flesh" (Hebrew basar). Perhaps Peter is calling Balaam the "son of the flesh." "The way of Balaam" is a double entendre, referring to the sinful desire of Balaam as well as the literal path on which he rode the donkey, a path that he was forced to "wander off" because of the angel.

Balaam was, of course, the prophet whom the king of Moab tried to hire to curse Israel, according to Numbers 22–24. The Israelites were poised to enter Canaan, and Moab's king was terrified of them. Balaam wanted to receive the fee from the king, but he knew that he must first consult the Lord. The Lord first refused but later allowed him to go to the king of Moab. Apparently because of Balaam's wrong intentions (to curse Israel for money), God sent an angel to stop him, but only his donkey could see the angel. When the donkey turned off the road, crushed Balaam's foot, and finally stopped, he threatened the donkey, after which God opened his eyes to see the angel.

Balaam had long since become a standard negative example, in the Old Testament and in later Jewish literature (Deut 23:4-5; Josh 13:22; 24:9-10; Neh 13:1-2; Micah 6:5). Jewish tradition states what the Numbers narrative implies, that Balaam's sin was his desire to prophesy what the king desired in exchange for money.[16] Therefore the phrase, "the wages of wickedness," refers to the financial gain a prophet or teacher receives for speaking.

2:16 But he was rebuked for his wrongdoing by a donkey — a beast without speech — who spoke with a man's voice and restrained the prophet's madness.

The assumption is that Balaam had decided to prophesy against Israel for the money. So the "brute beast" (from verse 12) proved more reasonable than the man who, like the false teachers, was following his worst impulses. The donkey acts as the man should, and the man acts like the donkey, that is, irrationally ("madness").

4. The Future Suffering of the False Teachers (2:17-22)

[17]**These men are springs without water and mists driven by a storm. Blackest darkness is reserved for them.** [18]**For they mouth empty, boastful words and, by appealing to the lustful desires of sinful human nature, they entice people who are just escaping from those who live in error.** [19]**They**

---

[16]See Bauckham, *2 Peter*, p. 81, for a brief summary of the fascinating expansions of the story of Balaam in Jewish traditions.

promise them freedom, while they themselves are slaves of depravity — for a man is a slave to whatever has mastered him. [20]If they have escaped the corruption of the world by knowing our Lord and Savior Jesus Christ and are again entangled in it and overcome, they are worse off at the end than they were at the beginning. [21]It would have been better for them not to have known the way of righteousness, than to have known it and then to turn their backs on the sacred command that was passed on to them. [22]Of them the proverbs are true: "A dog returns to its vomit,"[a] and, "A sow that is washed goes back to her wallowing in the mud."

[a]22 Prov. 26:11

In this section Peter continues to attack the false teachers, especially with regard to their teaching of others. The emphasis is that their teaching leaves those who follow them even worse off than they were before becoming Christians. Peter's vivid metaphors reflect his attitude toward the false teachers.

2:17 These men are springs without water and mists driven by a storm. Blackest darkness is reserved for them.
Since water sustains life, water is a common metaphor for the teachings of God. Jesus speaks, for example, of the living water which he could give the Samaritan woman so that she would never thirst again (John 4:14). Peter accuses the false teachers of promising water but failing to deliver. They are like springs that have run dry and mists that are quickly blown away before they can refresh.

Since the last six words are exactly the same as those in Jude 13, many think that Peter is following Jude here. If so, he has altered the metaphor that in Jude referred to "wandering stars" forever consigned to darkness. Peter's reference to "darkness" is just like that which was common among Jews and Christians. For example, Jesus warns that some "will be thrown outside, into the darkness, where there will be weeping and gnashing of teeth" (Matt 8:12).

2:18 For they mouth empty, boastful words and, by appealing to the lustful desires of sinful human nature, they entice people who are just escaping from those who live in error.

Peter now explains how the false teachers are like springs and mists that promise water but cannot produce. They make great claims, but there is in fact nothing to them. Their success in reality comes from their appeal to the sinful desires of people. Here those desires are called "lustful," probably implying sexual desire. Unfortunately, those who are most likely to follow them are recent converts who are not yet established in faith and practice. They are "enticed" back into the sinful ways of their former pagan friends ("those who live in error"). They have not yet had time to grow out of their desire for their former practices.

Perhaps a word is in order at this point about those who appeal to the worst in people in order to further their personal agendas. Modern Christian leaders who preach the health and wealth gospel would be good examples. Similarly, those who deny biblical teachings on sexual matters regarding premarital sex and homosexuality may also fall into this category.

2:19 They promise them freedom,

Peter now explains one of the boastful claims that these teachers have falsely made. Though empty, their promise of freedom must have sounded impressive and, in fact, very much like one of the great claims of the early Christians. Paul especially calls his churches to freedom in Christ, making such statements as, "It is for freedom that Christ has set us free" (Gal 5:1).

From the earliest times there have been Christians whose misunderstanding of God's grace has led them to be unconcerned about sin (see Rom 6:1-3). The false teachers opposed by Peter may have shared such a doctrine of grace, and they may have misread Paul's letters in order to support their understandings (see 3:16). However, their freedom from moral concerns was also related directly to their disbelief in the final judgment at the Second Coming of Christ. Their "no final judgment" doctrine led to their loose living.

while they themselves are slaves of depravity — for a man is a slave to whatever has mastered him.

The term φθόρα (*phthora*) translated "depravity" might also be translated "corruption," the destruction to be brought upon evildoers. In either case, Peter notes the irony that the so-called freedom of the false teachers actually leads to slavery. If Peter means that they have become slaves of (future) destruction, this is certainly true. However, he probably means that they have become enslaved by their sinful desires. The next statement concerning their having been "mastered" favors this view. This was most likely a well-known proverb in Peter's day. As applied to the false teachers, it means that they were no longer in control of their own lives, since their passions had taken charge.

2:20 If they have escaped the corruption of the world by knowing our Lord and Savior Jesus Christ and are again entangled in it and overcome, they are worse off at the end than they were at the beginning.

Peter continues to speak of *moral* corruption. But to whom does he refer when he writes, "they have escaped?" Are "they" the false teachers or those whom they are enticing? The Greek is ambiguous, as is the NIV. Although many modern commentators favor the false teachers, there are two reasons for thinking otherwise. First, this section returns to the idea introduced in verse 13 concerning the "harm" which these teachers are doing. Second, Peter has nowhere suggested that these false teachers ever lived holy lives that proclaimed Jesus Christ as Lord. It seems better to take verse 19 as a parenthetical comment, so that "they" in verse 20 refers to the "people who are just escaping" in verse 18. (Of course, this verse presents a terrible truth, no matter which group Peter has in mind.)

"Knowing" Jesus as "Lord and Savior," according to Peter, leads to freedom from the sinfulness of the world. But he knows that it is possible to become involved again in ungodly living. The terms "entangled" and "overcome" suggest how Christians often revert to earlier sins. It is rarely a conscious choice to do what is wrong. More often such Christians assume they can handle the situation, only to find themselves trapped and overpowered. Peter's primary point is found in the final words in this verse: those who return to lives dominated by sin are actually "worse off" than they were before becoming Christians. The English reader will probably miss the fact that these words are almost exactly those of Jesus in Matthew 12:45: "The final condition of that man is worse than the first." Jesus spoke these words at the end of his discussion about the evil spirit that left a man but then found no better place to live. When it returned and found its former home unoccupied, it brought seven other worse spirits to live there, too. Peter's use of Jesus' words is further explained in verse 21.

2:21 It would have been better for them not to have known the way of righteousness, than to have known it and then to turn their backs on the sacred command that was passed on to them.

Restating in stronger terms what he has just written, Peter argues that they would be better off if they had never experienced the Christian life than to "turn their backs" on holy living. The general import of the statement is clear — it would be better at the judgment never to have been a Christian, because God will punish more severely those who knew the truth but gave it up.

The phrase "the way of righteousness" recalls the earlier phrases, "the way of truth" in 2:2 and "the straight way" in 2:15. All three refer to the "way" of holy living. The "sacred command that was passed on to them" refers most likely to the command to live lives of holiness, rather than any of the

specific instructions they were given when they became
Christians.

**2:22 Of them the proverbs are true: "A dog returns to its
vomit," and, "A sow that is washed goes back to her wallowing in the mud."**

The final statements in this section are Peter's quotation
of two well-known and distasteful proverbs. Both involve animals that were unclean to Jews and generally regarded as dis-
gusting by all. This is the third comparison in this chapter of
unholy lives to the ways of animals (see verses 12 and 16). The
point of the analogy is painfully obvious.

2 PETER 3

C. THE NECESSITY OF BELIEVING IN CHRIST'S RETURN (3:1-13)

1. The False Teaching (3:1-7)

¹Dear friends, this is now my second letter to you. I have written both of them as reminders to stimulate you to wholesome thinking. ²I want you to recall the words spoken in the past by the holy prophets and the command given by our Lord and Savior through your apostles.

³First of all, you must understand that in the last days scoffers will come, scoffing and following their own evil desires. ⁴They will say, "Where is this 'coming' he promised? Ever since our fathers died, everything goes on as it has since the beginning of creation." ⁵But they deliberately forget that long ago by God's word the heavens existed and the earth was formed out of water and by water. ⁶By these waters also the world of that time was deluged and destroyed. ⁷By the same word the present heavens and earth are reserved for fire, being kept for the day of judgment and destruction of ungodly men.

As Peter begins to close his letter, he returns to his earlier emphasis on strengthening the faith of his readers. He reminds them of the many reasons for believing that Jesus is indeed coming back in judgment. It is here that he most clearly reveals the arguments of the false teachers. They teach that Christ will not return, because he has not yet returned as expected, and because the world has continued without change since the creation. Peter reminds the readers that God created the world by his word, then destroyed the world by his word, and that he certainly can and will destroy it again by his word. Destruction awaits the ungodly.

3:1 Dear friends, this is now my second letter to you. I have written both of them as reminders to stimulate you to wholesome thinking.

Peter seems to know his readers well, as he calls them "loved ones" (ἀγαπητοί, *agapētoi*). (The NIV's "friends" is not strong enough.) Since he calls this his "second" letter to these Christians, it is probable that the first was the letter we call 1 Peter. This is not certain, though, since 1 Peter could have been sent to a different group of Christians. Peter probably wrote many more letters than these two.[1]

His purpose for both, "to stimulate you to wholesome thinking," is stated very generally. Since both letters deal with the ethical obligations of Christians, the description is an accurate one. The term translated "wholesome" refers to purity or a lack of contamination. Peter's fear at the time of this writing is, of course, that the false teachers will contaminate the thinking of his readers.

3:2 I want you to recall the words spoken in the past by the holy prophets and the command given by our Lord and Savior through your apostles.

Just as he did in 1:16-21, Peter reminds these believers that his words are based on the words of the prophets and the apostles, who passed on what Jesus taught them. He speaks of "your apostles," probably referring to the apostles who first taught these readers.

---

[1]Those who think that Peter did not write this letter find in this statement clear evidence that the writer is trying too hard to sound like Peter. But it is not at all unlikely that Peter would refer to an earlier letter.

The content of the "words" and the "command" is some-what difficult to determine. Peter may be discussing the demand for holy living preached by the prophets and by Jesus. The word "command" (ἐντολή, *entolē*) would seem to support this view. Yet he may be looking forward to the fol-lowing verse, suggesting that the prophets and Jesus predict-ed that false teachers would come and lead people into apos-tasy. Or he may be writing about the future coming of Jesus in judgment, also taught by the prophets and by Jesus him-self. This would be supported by the primary teaching of the whole letter, especially the similar section in 1:16-21. It is impossible to rule out any of these as possibilities, and it may be best to assume Peter has in mind all three. Jesus and the prophets spoke of the need for holy living to escape the final judgment at the final coming of God's Messiah. They also knew that some would deny these truths.

3:3 First of all, you must understand that in the last days scoffers will come, scoffing and following their own evil desires.

The phrase, "first of all," indicates that these Christians must first understand that Jesus and the prophets knew of these "scoffers" long ago. In other words, Peter's readers should not be alarmed or swayed by these men — they knew they were coming. As discussed above, Peter may use the future tense here (scoffers *will* come) because the false teach-ers have only begun their destructive program, which will get worse. Or it may be that he is in essence quoting the words of Jesus and the prophets to which he has just alluded. Matthew 24:5 is a good example: "Many will come in my name, claim-ing, 'I am the Christ,' and will deceive many."

The words, "in the last days," have been taken in two differ-ent ways. Some think that this writer believes that the final days are just arriving at this time, the false teachers themselves being the proof. However, the most common understanding

in the New Testament is that Jesus inaugurated the last days
and that all Christians are therefore living in the last days. It
does not refer to the last *few* days before the end but rather
the last period of history in terms of God's dealings with
humans.

Throughout the Bible, "scoffers" are those who ridicule
the teachings of God. They tend to discount the spiritual
world, making their judgments based on worldly wisdom. In
this case they are ridiculing the idea of the Second Coming.
Peter ties their scoffing to their sinful lifestyles — they scoff at
God's ways and follow "their own evil desires."

**3:4 They will say, "Where is this 'coming' he promised? Ever
since our fathers died, everything goes on as it has since the
beginning of creation."**

The form of the ridicule of the false teaching is a fairly
common one in the Old Testament. Peter's use of this form
puts these men in the same category as those who asked
Jeremiah, for example, "Where is the word of the Lord? Let it
now be fulfilled!" The question, "Where is this 'coming'?" is
asked with sarcasm, and it means, "He did not return as he
said he would, did he?"

The last part of the verse, the reasoning behind the scoffing, is subject to two major interpretations. The first is that
there will be no complete destruction of the world because
such a thing never has happened — not since the beginning of
the world. (This interpretation will be discussed below.) The
second and most common interpretation among modern commentators is that the scoffers contended that Jesus promised
to come back during the lifetime of his early disciples. They
would have gotten this idea from such passages as Matthew
16:28: "I tell you the truth, some who are standing here will
not taste death before they see the Son of Man coming in
his kingdom." It is just such an expectation that has led
the false teachers to mention the death of "our fathers."
According to this view the "fathers" here must be the fathers

of the Christian faith, the earliest generation of disciples or even the apostles themselves.[2]

This view is not without merit. It is at least understandable that believers would think that Jesus promised to return before the death of some who were present during his ministry. After the early disciples died, the mockery was inevitable. However, there are a few problems with this reading. First, it is not at all clear that Jesus promised to return during the lifetime of his disciples. The texts that may appear to teach this are certainly subject to other understandings. Not only have they been interpreted in other ways for 1,900 years; it is also quite doubtful that the Gospel writers so understood them as they penned these words toward the end of that first generation.

Second, the term "fathers" is nowhere else used to describe the early Christians.[3] It is often used, however, to speak of the Old Testament "fathers of the faith," as in Romans 9:5; 11:28; 15:8; Acts 7:2,32. There the term refers to Abraham and his near descendants. The phrase, "since the beginning of creation," also leads the reader to assume the fathers are the ancient heroes of the faith because it is parallel to the phrase "since our fathers died."

Third, the writer (whether Peter or not) never really answers the charge that the early Christians have died before the return of Jesus. His answer is much better suited to the understanding of the scoffers' charges presented below. He answers that the Lord has reasons for waiting, not that the Lord never imposed a time limit or that he changed the limit. Surely the writer would have attempted to answer the question directly if he understood it that way.

---

[2]The pronoun "our" does not appear in the Greek text. The NIV may mislead readers into assuming (wrongly) that the scoffers are claiming a close temporal relationship to these fathers.

[3]Bauckham has to argue that "2 Peter seems to be unique in the literature of the first two Christian centuries" in this respect (p. 292).

The better view seems to be that which understands the term "our fathers" to refer to the Old Testament patriarchs, its more normal connotation. The scoffers' reasoning is, then, "It has been several decades now and Jesus still has not returned, as he promised. In fact, the world continues upon its course just the way it has since the time of Abraham. Only dreamers would think that it is about to change."

Unfortunately, we cannot know precisely what has led these false teachers to such a position. They apparently see themselves as Christians, so they must have respect for Jesus. It is, in fact, odd that they seem to deny the coming *he* promised. Perhaps it means "the coming that some say he promised." What has led them to deny the Second Coming? First, there is little doubt that their sinful lifestyles have influenced their thinking. It is a fact that behavior influences thinking as often as thinking influences behavior. Humans have an amazing ability to rationalize their behavior. But how did the false teachers support their denial of the Second Coming on an intellectual level? This verse may give the clearest hint, since Peter quotes them as contending that, "everything goes on as it has since the beginning of creation." Their statement seems to imply a philosophy of history. Perhaps these teachers blended Christianity with Greco-Roman philosophical thought. The Epicureans believed that the gods existed but that there was nothing to fear from them.[4] The gods could do nothing to hurt people. More likely, though, the false teachers were simply typical Greek thinkers who believed time moves in a continuous cycle and not toward an end. "Everything goes on as it has." The concept of an end to the world may not have made any sense to these people.[5] It has been that way

---

[4]Jerome Neyrey, *2 Peter, Jude: A New Translation with Introduction and Commentary*. Anchor Bible (New York: Doubleday, 1993), thinks that the teaching of the false teachers is based on Epicurean philosophy. The Epicureans taught that death is not to be feared, since there is no reward or punishment in the afterlife.

[5]This is very difficult for modern conservative Christians even to under-

"since the beginning of creation," and it will always be that way.

Excursus: The Imminent Coming of Jesus

It must be admitted that the early Christians seem to have expected Jesus to return within a generation or so. This is the reason for the crisis at Thessalonica that Paul responds to in 1 Thessalonians 4:13-18. Some in that church became concerned when loved ones began to die and Jesus had not returned. This suggests that they expected him back by that time. It does not prove that he had promised to come back by that time. Paul's response is, of course, that the dead will be raised when Jesus returns, so that their loved ones would not miss out on Jesus' return.

A number of other New Testament texts also seem to assume that Jesus would be back "soon." In 1 Corinthians 7:29,31, Paul writes that, "The time is short. From now on those who have wives should live as if they had none; . . . For this world in its present form is passing away." James writes, "Be patient and stand firm, because the Lord's coming is near" (Jas 5:8).

There are several answers to this "problem." First, it must be remembered that Jesus said that, "No one knows about that day or hour, not even the angels in heaven, nor the Son, but only the Father. Be on guard! Be alert! You do not know when that time will come" (Mark 13:32). If the early church expected Jesus back during the first generation, it was their

---

stand. However, this sort of thinking was only too common in the early centuries. Some Christians in Corinth seemed to believe that the spiritual world was good and the physical world, including the body, was evil. This led some to deny all bodily desires and others to decide that the body is not the real self, so that sexual immorality was of no concern (see 1 Cor 6:12-20). Some Corinthians also denied the resurrection, thinking that the resurrection of the body was a foolish doctrine.

opinion and not inspired prophecy. Second, it may be that the New Testament writers were trying to convey the idea of imminence. That is, everything is ready for the Second Coming, so that it could arrive at any moment. In that sense it is "near." Third, the present passage in 2 Peter offers the most satisfying answer in the New Testament. If it seems that God is slow, it is not slowness but patience. And besides, human beings are incapable of understanding God's time-table. "With the Lord a day is like a thousand years, and a thousand years are like a day" (2 Pet 3:8).

3:5 But they deliberately forget that long ago by God's word the heavens existed and the earth was formed out of water and by water. 3:6 By these waters also the world of that time was deluged and destroyed.

Peter accuses these men of having a selective memory.[6] They "deliberately forget" that the world was created by "God's word," and that it was also by his word that it was destroyed. The point is that God can (and will) do it again. In other words, their assumption that the world will simply continue without change ignores two important facts: God created the world, and God once destroyed the world. That destruction by water serves as an example, a reminder and an assurance that God will again destroy the ungodly.

The statement that heaven and earth were formed "out of water and by water" is somewhat perplexing. Probably its meaning is that God formed the heavens and the earth *out of* "the deep" (Gen 1:2) and that he made them *by* water when he separated and gathered the waters. Separating the waters above from the waters below formed the sky (heavens), and

---

[6]The Greek is ambiguous here. The phrase translated, "they deliberately forget that," may also be translated, "in maintaining this, they overlook the fact that." It is difficult to decide which Peter meant, but it matters very little. In either case, the false teachers fail to consider what they know about God's creation of the world and its destruction in the flood.

gathering together the waters below created dry ground (Gen 1:6-10).[7]

Even if the precise meaning of the discussion of "water" here is difficult, the reason for it is clear enough. God once destroyed the world with water, but he will destroy it with fire the next time. And it too will be by the power of his word. A better translation for the NIV's "by these waters" would be simply "by these," referring to the waters *and* the word of God. Perhaps the false teachers doubted God's ability to bring about catastrophic change in the world. Peter assures his readers that God need only speak the word.

3:7 By the same word the present heavens and earth are reserved for fire, being kept for the day of judgment and destruction of ungodly men.

The all-powerful word of God has already decreed that "the present heavens and earth" will be destroyed by fire. Since God has spoken, it will occur. The only unknown factor is the time. The teaching that the world will be destroyed by fire is taught only here in the New Testament. Peter is very likely referring here to the words of the prophets, such as those of Malachi: "'Surely the day is coming; it will burn like a furnace. All the arrogant and every evildoer will be stubble, and that day that is coming will set them on fire,' says the LORD Almighty" (4:1). This passage from Malachi and others like it from the Old Testament do not envision a fiery destruction for the whole creation but rather only for ungodly people. In fact, only in 2 Peter is it taught that "the heavens and earth" will be consumed by fire. This undoubtedly looks forward to the "new heaven and new earth" of verse 13, where we will discuss it further.

The coming fiery day is "the day of judgment," when all will be judged. It will therefore also be the day of "destruction of ungodly men," such as the false teachers.

---

[7]Bauckham, *2 Peter*, p. 297.

2. The Sure Return of Christ (3:8-10)

[8]But do not forget this one thing, dear friends: With the Lord a day is like a thousand years, and a thousand years are like a day. [9]The Lord is not slow in keeping his promise, as some understand slowness. He is patient with you, not wanting anyone to perish, but everyone to come to repentance.

[10]But the day of the Lord will come like a thief. The heavens will disappear with a roar; the elements will be destroyed by fire, and the earth and everything in it will be laid bare.[a]

[a]*10* Some manuscripts *be burned up*

In this section Peter answers the false teachers' fundamental doctrinal error. There were very good reasons that Christ had not yet returned. But make no mistake — he will return, and the world as presently known will be no more.

3:8 But do not forget this one thing, dear friends: With the Lord a day is like a thousand years, and a thousand years are like a day.

In response to the scoffers' teaching that Jesus had not returned when expected, Peter offers his first response. He addresses his readers again as "loved ones" (*agapētoi*, not simply "friends") and encourages them not to "forget," as the false teachers "deliberately forget" (verse 5). He uses the language of Psalm 90:4, as he argues that the Lord does not view time as humans view time.[8]

---

[8]Bauckham, *2 Peter*, pp. 306-308, argues well that there is no reason to think that Peter is here writing about a 1,000-year "day" of judgment to come. For one thing, he insists that a day is "like" a thousand years, not that the day just spoken about "is" a thousand years. For another, such a reference would not in any way advance his argument about the delay of the Second Coming.

The fundamental thought here is that people, given their limited perspective, cannot possibly understand God's timetable. What seems an eternity to humans is only a brief moment to an eternal God. Several decades seemed to the early Christians a very long time to wait for the return of Jesus. In fact, Peter implies, this may be a very short time from God's perspective.

It is unusual that Peter writes not only that "a thousand years are like a day" (as in Psalm 90:4) but also that "a day is like a thousand years." The reversed statement (which is the first) is probably just for rhetorical effect. However, it is possible that Peter means that God delays too long in the eyes of some, and that God acts too quickly in the eyes of others.

3:9 The Lord is not slow in keeping his promise, as some understand slowness. He is patient with you, not wanting anyone to perish, but everyone to come to repentance.

Peter now explains *why* it is that the Lord has not yet returned. While from a human perspective he seems "slow in keeping his promise," the apparent delay has nothing to do with being slow. The "some" who accuse God of "slowness" are undoubtedly the scoffing teachers.

Far from showing a lack of concern for people, the Lord is actually showing mercy. The theme is a common one in the Old Testament, as time and again God waits to execute his judgment in order to give people a chance to repent. Joel 2:13 provides an excellent example: "Return to the LORD your God, for he is gracious and compassionate, slow to anger and abounding in love, and he relents from sending calamity." Peter does not deny that from a human point of view the return of Jesus seems delayed; but that apparent delay is actually patience, allowing for repentance.

The statement that God does not want "anyone to perish, but everyone to come to repentance," has always created problems for certain theologians. Those who believe that God has chosen some to be saved (and not others) have trouble explaining why God wants all to be saved but has chosen only some. A standard response is to ask who is actually included by the words "anyone" and "everyone." Since Peter writes that God is patient "with *you*," suggesting that some of his readers were in need of repentance, it is argued that Peter means "any of you" and "all of you." That is, God wants all those he has chosen to repent and therefore shows patience in sending Jesus. However, it must be noted that some are apparently in real danger of being caught unrepentant when Christ comes "as a thief in the night." And it is far from clear that "anyone" and "everyone" refer to God's chosen ones. For what sense does it make to say that God wants his saved ones to repent so they can be saved? Surely it is more reasonable to think that God wants everyone to repent and be saved.

As explained above, Peter does use the language of "election" in order to reassure his readers (see comments on 1:3). However, this letter as a whole tends to resonate better with a free-will doctrine rather than that of predestination.

3:10 But the day of the Lord will come like a thief.

If Peter has hinted that God has delayed his promised activity (and that is debatable), he wants to ensure that all know that the delay will not last. The verb "will come" begins the sentence in Greek. Christ will return, and he will do so at an unexpected time.

The term "day of the Lord" is an Old Testament phrase, commonly used by the prophets to speak of the coming judgment against sinful people and salvation for the people of God. In the New Testament it is used, as here, to warn of the return of Christ (1 Thess 5:4; Rom 2:5). The fact that it "will come like a thief" is based on Jesus' use of this metaphor (see Matt 24:43; Luke 12:39). The idea is, of course, that the thief breaks into the house when he is unexpected. Here it has great importance because it is the answer to the question of the scoffers (v. 4). The passage of time has led them not to *expect* the Second Coming. They will be surprised by the one who will come like a thief.

The heavens will disappear with a roar; the elements will be destroyed by fire, and the earth and everything in it will be laid bare.

Returning to the earlier teaching that all will be destroyed by fire, Peter envisions the "roar" of the flames that will consume "the heavens." Jesus spoke of the future passing away of the heavens and the earth (Matt 5:18; 24:35), and Peter most likely gets this teaching from him. He also clearly alludes to Isaiah 34:4: "All the stars of the heavens will be dissolved and the sky rolled up like a scroll; all the starry host will fall like withered leaves from the vine . . . ." Here "the heavens" probably refer to the physical heavens, most likely the sky, rather than the abode of God. "The elements" (στοιχεῖα, *stoicheia*) are best understood to refer to the heavenly bodies, such as the sun, moon, and stars. The fact that they will "melt" (v. 12) seems to support this understanding. It also seems to recall Isaiah 34:4 with its dissolved stars.

After describing both areas above the earth (sky and space), Peter speaks of what will happen to the earth itself. Oddly, he writes that "the earth and everything in it will *be laid bare.*"[9] Assuming that the image of a fiery destruction is still in Peter's mind, it is probable that he is writing about refinement, or purification by fire (see 1 Pet 1:7). The fire will determine what is pure and what is not. (Paul uses similar imagery in 1 Corinthians 3:13.)

---

[9]Some manuscripts have a different word than that translated "laid bare" in the NIV. For example, the NASB accepts as original the Greek word for "burned up," which is what the reader might expect in light of the previous verses in this chapter. But why would copyists have changed an easy reading to a difficult one? The NIV translators have made the right choice, since they have followed the best manuscripts and followed the more difficult reading.

3. Christian Living in Light of Christ's Return (3:11-13)

[11]Since everything will be destroyed in this way, what kind of people ought you to be? You ought to live holy and godly lives [12]as you look forward to the day of God and speed its coming.[a] That day will bring about the destruction of the heavens by fire, and the elements will melt in the heat. [13]But in keeping with his promise we are looking forward to a new heaven and a new earth, the home of righteousness.

[a]12 Or *as you will wait eagerly for the day of God to come*

After reminding them of the coming destruction of the ungodly, Peter now calls on his readers to live in light of the future. His message is not only about fear of punishment but is also about the joy of the new heaven and new earth.

3:11 Since everything will be destroyed in this way, what kind of people ought you to be? You ought to live holy and godly lives

The use of rhetorical questions has always been popular with those who call on others to do what is right. Peter not only asks the obvious question — he answers it. The thinking is the same as that of the prophets, Paul and most other New Testament writers, and Jesus (see especially the parable of the wise and foolish virgins in Matthew 25:1-13). Since the world will be destroyed and the faithfulness of everyone will be clearly shown, Christians must live "holy" and "godly" lives. Both of these terms are plural in Greek, signifying the many holy behaviors and godly acts to which believers are called.

3:12 as you look forward to the day of God and speed its coming.

A focus on the eternal future that begins with the return of Jesus provides motivation for Christian living. What is most encouraging about this verse is that it moves beyond simply using fear of judgment as motivation. Peter calls on all his readers to anticipate eagerly the "day of God" and even to *hasten* its coming. The "day of God" is obviously the day of judgment, the Second Coming of Christ, the end of the present world. But what does it mean to "speed its coming?" The word for "speed" could be simply a synonym for "look forward to," but it probably means more here. Peter has just written about God's patient waiting which is motivated by his desire to give people the time to repent. It is likely therefore that holy living is understood here to hasten the coming of Jesus. Luke records Peter speaking in a similar way in Acts 3:19-20: "Repent, then, and turn to God *so that* your sins may be wiped out, that times of refreshing may come from the Lord, and that he may send the Christ . . . ."[10]

That day will bring about the destruction of the heavens by fire, and the elements will melt in the heat.

Rehearsing what he has just written in verse 10, Peter writes that the day of God will be horrible and wonderful. It is unclear whether the phrase, "the heavens," refers to the sky or outer space or both. The "elements" are surely the stars, and they will "melt in the heat" (as in verse 10, see Isaiah 34:4).

3:13 But in keeping with his promise we are looking forward to a new heaven and a new earth, the home of righteousness.

God's promise is not only that this world and its wickedness will be destroyed. It is also that the new world will be "the home of righteousness." While lazy and discouraged Christians may need to be reminded of the coming punishment of the sinful, the greater motivation for Christians is God's promise of life with him. Peter borrows from Isaiah in order to express this future period. In Isaiah 65:17, God says, "Behold, I will create new heavens and a new earth." The picture is one in which sin has been conquered, and God's will is being done.

---

[10]See Moo, *2 Peter*, p. 198.

When many Christians think about eternal life, the thought is only of "heaven." Here Peter envisions not only a new heaven but also a new earth, presumably the dwelling place of God's people. Even though the picture of eternal life with God is necessarily fuzzy, it should be remembered that Christians look forward to the resurrection of the body and the redemption and renewal of the creation, which has been subjected to frustration (Rom 8:20).

III. FINAL EXHORTATIONS (3:14-18)

[14]So then, dear friends, since you are looking forward to this, make every effort to be found spotless, blameless and at peace with him. [15]Bear in mind that our Lord's patience means salvation, just as our dear brother Paul also wrote you with the wisdom that God gave him. [16]He writes the same way in all his letters, speaking in them of these matters. His letters contain some things that are hard to understand, which ignorant and unstable people distort, as they do the other Scriptures, to their own destruction.

[17]Therefore, dear friends, since you already know this, be on your guard so that you may not be carried away by the error of lawless men and fall from your secure position. [18]But grow in the grace and knowledge of our Lord and Savior Jesus Christ. To him be glory both now and forever! Amen.

Although it is arguable that the conclusion to the letter does not begin until verse 17, the repetitive nature of these verses may suggest that Peter is now summing up his practical advice. He also returns to the wording of the beginning of the letter, when he writes about the "knowledge of our Lord" (see 1:3) and their need to "make every effort" (see 1:5). Finally, he seems to mark the conclusion by the use of "so then, dear friends" in verse 14. The use of the similar "therefore, dear friends" in verse 17 serves to return to concluding remarks after the parenthetical statements about Paul.

3:14 So then, dear friends, since you are looking forward to this, make every effort to be found spotless, blameless and at peace with him.

After his third reference to these Christians as "loved ones" (NIV "dear friends"), Peter calls to their mind what he has just told them about the new heavens and earth. He reminds them that they will only enjoy this wonderful existence if they "make every effort," echoing his words in 1:5. There he called them to goodness, knowledge, self-control, and the like. Here he calls them to "be found spotless, blameless, and at peace with him." It is, of course, by the exercise of the former virtues that they will at the judgment be found innocent. There is apparently a legal metaphor at work here, that of a trial before a judge. There is also the background of the sacrificial system, in which only the animals "without spot or blemish" are accepted. (The careful reader remembers that the false teachers are "blots and blemishes," according to 2:13.) The terms "spotless" and "blameless" refer to being without sin. The desire to be "at peace" most likely refers to the relationship with God that comes from having sins forgiven in Christ and living in light of that forgiveness.

3:15 Bear in mind that our Lord's patience means salvation, just as our dear brother Paul also wrote you with the wisdom that God gave him.

Peter repeats again the important teaching that the so-called delay of the return of Jesus is due to God's patient desire for people to repent and therefore receive "salvation." Peter then alludes to the teaching of Paul, perhaps to remind these Christians that the false teachers stand not only against Peter but also against the apostle Paul. This probably implies that Paul was well known and respected among the Christians who received this letter. He was also *loved* by Peter and by others (perhaps these readers or other apostles), as indicated in the description "our dear ["loved," ἀγαπητός, *agapētos*] brother Paul." Peter may mean that Paul wrote specifically to these people ("Paul also wrote *you*"), in which case they would naturally think of Paul as dear or beloved.

Peter acknowledges the already common belief that Paul's "wisdom" came from God. This acceptance of Paul by Peter is one of the so-called proofs that Peter could not have written this letter. It is argued that Paul and Peter were on opposite sides in the early church, Peter representing a very Jewish approach and Paul a very non-Jewish approach. There certainly were some early troubles between these two over some matters (see Gal 2:11-14). However, there is every indication that these were quickly worked out and that Peter and Paul were of the same mind in all important areas. Not only does the book of Acts show Peter and Paul together at the Jerusalem council (Acts 15). They also were both helped by Silas (1 Pet 5:12; 1 Thess 1:1, etc.) and Mark (1 Pet 5:13; Col 4:10). The differences between Peter and Paul have been greatly overstated.

3:16 He writes the same way in all his letters, speaking in them of these matters.

Peter acknowledges what all readers of Paul's letters know.[11] In virtually every letter Paul calls his readers to a holy life, basing his exhortation on the coming of Christ. A typical example is Romans 13:11-13: "And do this, understanding the present time. The hour has come for you to wake up from your slumber, because our salvation is nearer now than when we first believed. The night is nearly over; the day is almost here. So let us put aside the deeds of darkness and put on the armor of light. Let us behave decently . . . ."

---

[11]There is no way to know how many of Paul's letters these Christians had collected. But there is no reason to think, as do some scholars, that Peter is alluding to a large collection. "All" simply means all that Peter knew.

His letters contain some things that are hard to understand, which ignorant and unstable people distort, as they do the other Scriptures, to their own destruction.

Having mentioned the letters of Paul, Peter now feels the need to deal with the fact that some are misusing Paul. That parts of Paul's letters are "hard to understand" would probably be agreed upon as quickly in the early church as in its modern counterpart. Not only did he write about specific situations which only the originally addressed church would fully comprehend, Paul also wrote things that were subject to misinterpretation. It is quite possible that the false teachers Peter opposed claimed Paul for their position. It could be that they misunderstood Paul's teachings on justification by faith and Christian freedom, using them to justify libertine behavior.[12] Paul himself had to counter this misuse of his teaching (Rom 6:1-2, Gal 5:13). In the second century, Gnostic heretics regularly cited Paul's writings.

Peter accuses those who "distort" Paul's writings of being "ignorant" and "unstable." The terms probably refer to the false teachers and may also refer to those who follow them. There is no hint here that these people are excused on the basis of their ignorance and instability since they are willfully so (see 3:5). This too will contribute to their coming "destruction."

It is especially interesting that Peter writes of the distortion of Paul's letters along with "the other Scriptures." The implication is that the letters of Paul were already regarded as Scripture at the time Peter wrote. While many have dated 2 Peter into the second century on this basis, there is no compelling reason to do so. It is quite reasonable to think that the letters of the apostles were regarded as Scripture almost immediately. Paul claims to be inspired and authoritative in

---

[12]It is also possible that these false teachers misinterpret and *reject* Paul's teaching rather than misinterpret and follow them. Since Paul clearly taught the resurrection and Second Coming of Jesus (for example, 1 Thess 4:13-18), it would be interesting to know how they dealt with such teaching.

his letters, which may have been read during the assembly (see Col 4:16).

3:17 Therefore, dear friends, since you already know this, be on your guard so that you may not be carried away by the error of lawless men and fall from your secure position.

With the words, "Therefore, dear friends" (see 3:14), Peter returns to his concluding remarks after his aside about the letters of Paul. He has given them no new information in this letter but has rather "reminded them" (1:12; 3:1-2) of what they already knew from the prophets, apostles, and Jesus himself. They are to "be on guard," because the false teachers sound impressive (2:18-19) and because *many* will follow them (2:2). These men are "lawless," since their lack of moral constraint has led them into lust and greed (2:13-15).

Christians can be confident in their relationship with God ("secure position") by putting their complete confidence in Jesus and living in light of God's holiness. However, it is possible to "fall" from that high position by failing to strive for holiness. It is especially dangerous to be surrounded by people who are encouraging sinful living. Therefore Peter ends this letter as he began it, with an exhortation for spiritual growth (1:5-8; 3:18).

3:18 But grow in the grace and knowledge of our Lord and Savior Jesus Christ. To him be glory both now and forever! Amen.

The antidote to being "carried away" is to "grow in the grace and knowledge" of Christ. Peter described this process early in this letter by encouraging his readers to add to their faith goodness, knowledge, self-control, perseverance, godliness, brotherly kindness, and love (1:5-7). These are all gifts that can only come from the grace of God. However, only those who seek these gifts will receive them. The exhortation to "grow" means to "make every effort" (1:5).

One Christian virtue, knowledge, is singled out by Peter for special mention. Peter has already written several times of the importance of knowledge (1:2,3,8; 2:20). This is because the false teachers' fundamental error is a lack of knowledge. Their wrong thinking about the return of Christ has had disastrous consequences for their lives. Bad thinking leads to bad living. Correct thinking encourages right living.

Peter ends the letter with a doxology to Christ. Although many Jewish and Christian writings ended with doxologies, it is somewhat unusual to end a letter in this way (but see Philippians 4:20 and Romans 16:25-27). It is even more unusual to find a doxology to Jesus Christ rather than to God the Father (but see 2 Timothy 4:18 and Revelation 1:4-6). However, given Peter's very high view of Jesus (see comments on 1:1), it is not surprising.

"To him be glory" is a prayer that Jesus will be praised. The NIV translation "both now and forever" obscures the reference to "the day of the ages" in the original. Given the content of 2 Peter, the reference may be to the day that will begin with the Second Coming of Jesus.

Peter's final words provide a fitting prayer with which to end these comments on his letter: "Lord, may we continually grow in the grace and knowledge of our Lord and Savior Jesus Christ. To him be glory both now and forever! Amen."